Jesus

Introducing His Life and Teaching

Rev. Leonard F. Badia, Ph.D

Jesus

Introducing His Life and Teaching

Paulist Press
New York/Mahwah

Library of Congress
Catalog Card Number: 84-62565

ISBN: 0-8091-2689-3

Published by Paulist Press
997 Macarthur Boulevard
Mahwah, N.J. 07430

Printed and bound in the
United States of America

Contents

1. The Historical Jesus   1

2. Jesus the Person   16

3. The New Testament Writings'
   Portrait of Jesus   38

4. The Resurrection   67

5. Jesus' Humanity and Divinity   89

6. The Shroud of Turin   113

7. The Dead Sea Scrolls   136

8. Jesus' Human Knowledge   153

9. Special Biblical Questions about Jesus   176

*Dedicated to
my wonderful mother, Madeline,
who showed her children, Donatus, Theresa,
Elaine, and Leonard how to love, console, laugh, forgive,
trust and pray*

1

The Historical Jesus

The entrance of Jesus into the world changed the course of history. Many people have viewed him differently. All Muslims acknowledge that Jesus was a prophet and a messenger of God. Many Muslims believe that Jesus will return to earth before the final judgment, conquer evil forces and usher in the reign of God. The Hindus today accept the divinity of Jesus, but not that he is unique. Generally speaking, Marxists reject all gods including Jesus Christ. For Lenin, Jesus never existed and was a mythical invention. However, since the late 1960s, among the Marxists, there has been a revived interest in Jesus. First, there is an acknowledgment that he existed. Second, neo-Marxists are solely interested in his social messages. Other groups also have an opinion about Jesus. Of course, for Christians, he is the Son of God, truly human and divine.

Yet there have been people who have asked: How do we know that Jesus ever existed? The existence of Jesus outside of the writings of the New Testament is mentioned by three Roman writers, Suetonius, Tacitus and Pliny the Younger, and by the Jewish historian Josephus.

Non-Christian Sources

1. Suetonius (*Life of Emperor Claudius* 25:4) mentioned the expulsion of Jews from Rome in A.D. 49 because of their riots at the instigation of Chrestus. Suetonius wrote around A.D. 120 and, like many Romans, considered Christians and Jews as members of the same religious sect. What is most significant in this piece of evidence is the point that by the middle of the first century, a strong testimony to Christ was made in the capital of the Roman Empire (Rome).

2. Another Roman writer, Pliny the Younger (*Epistle* 10:96ff), who was governor of Asia Minor, wrote a letter to the Emperor Trajan (c. A.D. 111). He asked for advice in the matter of dealing with Christians who come together at fixed seasons and sing hymns to Christ as a god.

3. Finally, the Roman historian Tacitus, in his *Annals* 15:44, which was written around A.D. 110, stated: "They got their name from Christ, who was executed by sentence of the procurator Pontius Pilate in the reign of Tiberius. That checked the pernicious superstition for a short time, but it broke out afresh not in Judea, where the plague first arose, but in Rome itself where all horrible and shameful things in the world collect and find a home."

This passage reveals Tacitus' account of the great fire which swept through the city of Rome in A.D. 64 during the reign of Emperor Nero. Nero blamed the Christians for the fire and so put to death many Christians. The value of Tacitus' writing is that he did not secure his information about Jesus' death from a Christian source. Tacitus did not use Jesus' proper name; he used the word Christ, the religious title which was used by Christians outside of Palestine as a proper title for Jesus.

4. The Jewish historian, Josephus, wrote the history of his people and the Jewish-Roman war (A.D. 66–70). In his work, *Antiquities* 20,200, he wrote: "James the brother of Jesus who was called the Christ. . . ." This passage was in reference to the stoning death of James who was an apostle of Jesus.

The non-Christian sources give us scanty information about Jesus. However, they do establish that Jesus existed, died and had followers. Our main source of the historical Jesus comes from the New Testament writings and early Christian writings: (1) the testimony of the Synoptic Gospels, (2) the testimony of St. John's Gospel, (3) the testimony of the Acts of the Apostles, (4) the testimony of Paul's letters, (5) the testimony of tradition.

Christian Sources

1. The Testimony of the Synoptic Gospels (A.D. 60–90)

The Synoptic Gospels (Matthew, Mark, Luke) basically speak of faith in Jesus Christ as the Messiah who offers salvation to all peoples. These Gospels reveal the sayings, parables, sermons, miracles and stories about Jesus. These accounts were written approximately between A.D. 60 and 90.

The simple vital statistics about Jesus are few. According to Matthew and Luke, he was born in Bethlehem about 8 or 6 B.C. Certainly, it was before the death of King Herod (4 B.C.). All the Synoptic Gospels give an account of Jesus' suffering and death in Jerusalem. While his death has been traditionally placed at A.D. 33, it took place sometime within Pontius Pilate's term as governor of Judea (A.D. 26–36). Jesus was born of Mary, a young

Jewish woman, who married Joseph. Because Joseph was a carpenter, he would be considered middle class by today's standards. The Gospels indicate that Jesus lived in Nazareth as an adolescent and young man (Lk 2:51–52). His public ministry began when he was about thirty years old (Lk 3:23). In preparation for his mission, he went into the Dead Sea area to think, pray, and form his plans (Mt 4:1–11; Mk 1:12–13; Lk 4:1–13). He was kind, gentle, articulate, strong, respectful, and prayerful and he taught with authority (Mt 7:28; Mk 1:22; Lk 4:15).

According to the Gospel of Mark, Jesus began his public ministry in the towns and villages of Galilee. He spoke in synagogues, in private homes, and on the lake shore. He characterized himself as the servant of God.

According to the Gospel of Matthew, Jesus spoke many times as a teacher. Matthew reports Jesus' ideas about the Kingdom of heaven and messiahship.

According to the Gospel of Luke, Jesus' humanity is emphasized. In particular, Jesus is mentioned as a friend of sinners, outcasts and the generally rejected members of society. Luke speaks of Jesus' parents, his birth, his boyhood and manhood. More than half of the stories about Jesus tell how he healed the sick of diseases like fever, leprosy, paralysis, blindness, deafness and dumbness.

The Gospels of Matthew, Mark and Luke are often called "Synoptic Gospels" because of the general agreement among them in structure, content and form about the events of Jesus' life.

2. The Testimony of St. John's Gospel (A.D. 90–100)

John's Gospel differs in content, plan and structure from the Snyoptic Gospels. In relationship with the Synoptic Gospels, John's Gospel has only the following common elements: the baptism of Jesus, the cleansing of the temple, the miracle of the loaves, the walking on the water, the anointing at Bethany, the triumphal entry into Jerusalem, the betrayal of Jesus, and the passion and resurrection of Jesus. It was written to complete the Synoptic accounts which were already in existence by the time John wrote his work. Basically, John's Gospel presents Jesus as the "Son of God." He is the "Word," the "Light," the "Life," and the "Son." He is the God-Man.

The key themes in John's Gospel are: (1) Jesus' preexistence, (2) Jesus' gift of life (Eucharist), (3) Jesus' central message of love, and (4) Jesus' Spirit (the Paraclete).

The unique differences of the four Gospel writers are: (1) Matthew writes for a Jewish audience, (2) Mark writes for a Roman audience, (3) Luke writes for a Greek audience, and (4) John writes for everyone (Jewish and non-Jewish people). Each writer presented aspects of Jesus' messages which would be appealing to his audience.

3. The Testimony of the Acts of the Apostles (A.D. 80–85)

Luke the writer of the third Gospel is also the author of the Acts of the Apostles. This book gives a great source of information about the two key leaders of the Christian movement, Peter and Paul. Both men were dedicated to spreading the messages of Jesus. Luke mentions the problems that these men had to deal with, but also gives an insight into their personalities.

The central message of the Acts of the Apostles is stated in chapter 1, verse 8: "You shall receive power when the the Holy Spirit has come upon you, and you shall be my (Jesus') witness in Jerusalem and in all Judea and in Samaria, and to the end of the earth." This writing reveals the existence of Jesus and the spread of his message, especially by Peter and Paul. Jesus' message spreads first to Jerusalem (chapters 1–7), then to Judea and Samaria (chapters 8–12), and finally to other parts of the world (chapters 13–28). It records the birth of the Church (chapter 2), the first deacons (chapter 6), the first martyr (chapter 7), the conversion of Paul (chapter 9), the first general council (chapter 15), and Paul's trips (chapters 13–21). Its key themes are: (1) Jesus is the servant of God (3:13—4:27); (2) Jesus is the judge of the living and dead (10:42; 17:30); (3) Jesus is the Savior (5:31)

4. The Testimony of St. Paul's Letters (A.D. 50–64)

Paul, a Jew born in Tarsus, Cilicia (A.D. 5–10) became a convert of Jesus. Because of his zeal for Jesus, he made three major trips (A.D. 45–59) throughout Asia Minor (Greece and Turkey). He became the apostle to the Gentiles (non-Jews). He brought Jesus' message to the Gentile world. His writings are the earliest writings of the New Testament period.

There are four key themes in Paul's letters. First, Jesus is the Lord (1 Cor 12:3; 2 Thes 1:9; Heb 1:10; Rom 10:13; Phil 2:10). For Paul, Jesus is the Lord, the mediator between God and man. It is the most common Pauline title for Jesus. In the Old Testament, the term "Lord" was applied to God. So, it became clear that Paul is saying that Jesus is God when he applies this title to him. Second, Jesus is the "last Adam" (1 Cor 15:45; Rom 5:15–21; Eph 2:15). Paul sees Jesus as the "first born of all creation" (1 Cor 1:15) and therefore the new responsible head of all mankind. Third, Jesus is the source of salvation for Jew and non-Jew. Fourth, Jesus has fulfilled the old law.

5. The Testimony of the Early Tradition of the Church (A.D. 100–200)

The oldest Church tradition acknowledges Jesus as the God-Man. The Apostles' Creed states that Jesus Christ is the Son of God. The earliest document of the second century, the *Didache*, mentions Christ to be the Lord (10:6), the God of David (10:6), and the Son of God (16:4).

Second, the testimony of Irenaeus (*Against Heresies* 3, 3, 3) says that Clement of Rome (c. A.D. 96) designated Christ as the Lord.

Third, Ignatius of Antioch (c. A.D. 107) proclaimed faith in Christ. He affirms the humanity of Jesus (*Smyrna* 10.1). He also affirms Jesus' divinity (*Smyrna* 10.1).

Fourth, Melito of Sardis (c. A.D. 120) speaks of the Godhead and manhood of Christ (*Paschal Homily* 8).

From these sample accounts of the second century, the Christian faith stressed the Godhead and manhood of Jesus. The *Didache*'s importance is that it reflects the life of a primitive Christian community somewhere in Syria or possibly Egypt toward the close of the first century. This community had accepted the existence of Jesus.

The writings of Irenaeus, Ignatius and Melito clearly dispel any doubt that Jesus was an historical person.

The Country of Jesus

Jesus, like his fellow countrymen and women, had lived under foreign occupation for some five hundred years since returning to their own land. By 63 B.C., the Roman general Pompey incorporated Palestine into the Roman province of Syria. The years 63–37 B.C. saw the definitive establishment of the Roman power in Palestine. And so, Jesus was born in Palestine when it was under the rule of the Roman Empire.

The name Palestine is originally derived from the Hebrew word *Pelishtim*, "the land of the Philistines." Eventually the Romans named the area Syria Palestina.

It has natural borders. There is the Mediterranean Sea on the west, the Egyptian desert on the south, the Syrian desert on the east, and the mountain area of Hermon on the north. The total area of Palestine is 15,000 square miles (about the size of Rhode Island). The length is 150 miles, the width 100 miles.

The geological characteristics vary: valleys, mountains, plains and bodies of water. Of special note are the two bodies of water where Jesus spent some of his time. The first, Lake Genesareth (also called the Sea of Galilee or Tiberias), is thirteen miles long and seven miles wide. Capernaum, one of Jesus' favorite towns, is situated on its shores. The second, the Dead Sea, is forty-seven miles long and ten miles wide. Some archaeologists believe that the cities of Sodom and Gomorrah are submerged under its waters. John the Baptist preached in this area. Jesus walked along its shores.

The climate varies according to the terrain. Basically, there are two seasons Jesus would have experienced. The summer is hot and dry. On days when the desert wind (*Khamsin*) blows from Arabia, the heat is intense. When the winds blow from the seacoast reaching cities like Jerusalem, it is very comfortable. The winter is wet, especially during the months of October, November, March and April. Despite loss of rain during June, July, August and September, there is sufficient water.

Politically, the Romans allowed the Jews to have a certain amount of autonomy. Herod the Great was the first Jewish king since Solomon to unite all Palestine under one rule. His jurisdiction covered nearly all of western Palestine, that is, the provinces of Idumea, Judea, Samaria, and Galilee. Jesus was born in the reign of Emperor Augustus (27 B.C.–A.D. 14) and King Herod the Great (37–4 B.C.). When Herod died in 4 B.C., Palestine was divided into three parts, one part for each of Herod's sons. Archelaus (4 B.C.–A.D. 6) ruled Samaria, Judea, and northern Idumea; Herod Antipas (4 B.C.–A.D. 39) ruled Galilee and Perea; Herod Philip (4 B.C.–A.D. 34) ruled Batanea. Because of Archelaus' incompetence, the Emperor Augustus removed him and appointed Pontius Pilate (A.D. 26–36) as governor of Judea.

While Palestine during Jesus' time was semi-independent to an extent, it was without doubt under the tight fist of Roman power. Jesus lived and died under Roman occupation. He lived under the reigns of Emperor Augustus of the Herod family and the Roman governor, Pontius Pilate. He died under the reigns of Emperor Tiberius and Pontius Pilate.

The Political-Religious Parties

Although Judaism is often referred to as a single type of religious belief and practice, there was not complete agreement among Jews of Jesus' time concerning doctrine or morals. There were several sects (parties) within Judaism itself. These sects were basically political-religious parties. The largest and most influential of these sects were the Pharisees. They not only required strict observance of the law (the torah) of Moses, but also emphasized the importance of the oral law as the source of their religion. They were headed by men who had high intellectual qualities, piety and moral rectitude. They believed in the immortality of the soul, freedom of the will, the resurrection of the body, future retribution, the existence of angels and divine providence. They also expected a Messiah who would establish an earthly kingdom. Finally, they held God to be a legislator and judge rather than a fatherly figure.

In many sections of the New Testament writings, the Pharisees were severely criticized by Jesus for their self-righteousness and legalism. While some were of this type, many were not. Both Nicodemus and Paul were Pharisees.

The Sadducees were another sect, smaller in number than the Pharisees, but very influential in politics. In some respects they were a conservative group since they held a strict and literal interpretation of the written law in the first five books of the Old Testament. They denied the immortality of the soul, the resurrection of the body, future retribution and the existence of the angels. Most Sadducees were of the aristocratic and priestly families. Jesus rarely came into conflict with them except for his warning against the bad leaven of both the Pharisees and Sadducees (Mt 16:6–11).

A third sect was known as the Essenes. This group produced the famous Dead Sea Scrolls which were discovered in 1947. A smaller and more exclusive sect than the Pharisees, they were formed to protect against the Greek influence on the Jewish religion, against corrupt kings and against the careless observance of the law. Because of their strict religious attitude, they generally withdrew from the large cities and lived in small towns and villages. The largest settlement group lived in the area of Qumran on the Dead Sea shores approximately sixteen miles east of Jerusalem. John the Baptist and James the apostle belonged to the Essene community.

Besides these three sects, there were smaller and less influential groups. One of these was known as the Zealots. They were extreme Jewish nationalists. They believed in violence. The Romans feared them because of their tendency to stir up rebellion against them. Eventually their fanatical hatred of the Romans led to the unsuccessful revolt against the Romans in A.D. 66–70. Simon the Zealot, one of Jesus' disciples, was a Zealot.

While the scribes were not a sect or a political party, they were important people. Generally speaking, the rabbis of today are the successors of the scribes. The scribes were the lawyers. Their principal functions were three-fold: legislative, judicial and instructive. Their legislative duties were to harmonize the theoretical and practical application of the law. Because of their judicial background, they were judges. Many of them were members of the Sanhedrin. They lectured on the Law. Paul the apostle was a pupil of the famous scribe Gamaliel (Acts 22:3).

Summary

1. The principal non-Christian sources for the proof of Jesus' existence are: the Roman writers, Suetonius, Pliny the Younger, and Tacitus, and the Jewish writer, Josephus.

2. The principal Christian sources of Jesus' existence are: the four Gospels, the Acts of the Apostles, Paul's letters, and the early writings of the Church.

3. The Synoptic Gospels (Matthew, Mark, Luke) were written between A.D. 60–90. They reveal the sayings, parables, sermons, miracles and stories of Jesus.

4. Mark's Gospel characterizes Jesus as the servant of God. Matthew's Gospel emphasizes Jesus' messianism. Luke's Gospel reveals primarily Jesus' humanity.

5. John's Gospel (A.D. 90–100) speaks of Jesus' divinity and his central message of love.

6. The Acts of the Apostles (A.D. 80–85) speaks of early Christianity's major leaders, Peter and Paul, and their spreading of Jesus' message throughout Palestine and Asia Minor (Greece and Turkey).

7. The key themes of Paul's letters are: Jesus is Lord; Jesus is Savior of Jew and non-Jew; Jesus fulfilled the old law; Jesus is the head of all followers who are Christians.

8. The early Church writings of Irenaeus, Ignatius and Melito establish the humanity of Jesus. The *Didache* document reflects the primitive Christian community's belief in Jesus' existence.

9. Palestine is 150 miles long, 100 miles wide. Its geological characteristics are: valleys, mountains, plains and bodies of water. Two of these water bodies are the Sea of Galilee and the Dead Sea.

10. Climatically, Palestine has two seasons: summer and winter. Politically in Jesus' time, Palestine was divided into three parts, each under a member of Herod's

family. Pontius Pilate was appointed by Rome to replace the incompetent Herod Archelaus.

11. Palestinian Judaism had three sects: Pharisees, Sadducees and Essenes. The Pharisees were rigorists. The Sadducees were conservatists. The Essenes were pacifists. Their religious doctrines differed.

12. Less influential groups were the Zealots and scribes. The Zealots were the extreme Jewish nationalists. The scribes were the lawyers.

Questions for Discussion

1. What is the Marxists' position on Jesus? From your general knowledge of Jesus' social messages, which ones would be appealing to Marxists?

2. State briefly the value of the non-Christian sources as a proof of the existence of Jesus.

3. What was the value of Tacitus' writing about Jesus?

4. Who are the Synoptic writers? When did they write? Why are they called Synoptic writers?

5. Which Synoptic writer in your opinion gives a better proof for the existence of Jesus? And why?

6. Why was John's Gospel written?

7. What is the central message of the Acts of the Apostles?

8. Read and discuss the Acts of the Apostles (3:13–4:27).

9. Why are Paul's letters so important in proving the existence of Jesus?

10. What is the *Didache* document?

11. Describe the political scene of Palestine during Jesus' time.

12. What are doctrinal differences of the Pharisees and Sadducees?

13. Do you think Jesus was a Pharisee or an Essene? Why?

14. Define: Zealots; Sadducees; Pharisees; scribes; Essenes.

Suggested Reading

P. Alexander, J. Drane, and D. Field, eds., *Eerdman's Family Encyclopedia of the Bible*. Grand Rapids: Wm. B. Eerdman's Publishing Co., 1978.

David and Pat Alexander, *The Lion Concise Bible Handbook*. England: Lion Publishing Co., 1980.

Joseph Fitzmyer, *A Christological Catechism: New Testament Answers*. New York/Ramsey: Paulist Press, 1982.

Neil Fujita, *Introducing the Bible*. New York/Ramsey: Paulist Press, 1981.

Charles Guignebert, *Jesus*. New York: University Books, 1956.

International Theological Commission, *Select Questions on Christology*. Washington, D.C.: United States Catholic Conference, 1980.

Joachim Jeremias, *Jerusalem in the Time of Jesus*. Philadelphia: Fortress Press, 1975.

John McKenzie, *Dictionary of the Bible*. Milwaukee: The Bruce Publishing Co., 1965.

2

Jesus the Person

Jesus' Life

Jesus was born in Bethlehem, Judea (the West Bank today) in the first century. He died under the Roman governor, Pontius Pilate, in the reign of Emperor Tiberius. The exact dates of Jesus' birth and death cannot be pinpointed exactly, but his life must fall between the death of Herod (4 B.C.) and A.D. 30. He was born of Jewish parents. When he was a young boy he lived in a town called Nazareth. It was a small place with about two hundred people. Like Joseph, his foster father, he learned to be a carpenter. Similar to his fellow countrymen and women, he lived under the power of the Roman Empire. Palestine was one of the many areas under the jurisdiction of Rome.

As a young man, Jesus attended the synagogue in Nazareth where he learned religious ideas from the rabbi. On the sabbath, as a faithful Jew, he went to the Jewish services. There he prayed, meditated and discussed the meaning of the Sacred Scriptures. He spoke and read Hebrew and common Aramaic.

When he was about thirty years old, he started to

preach and teach in many towns of Galilee and other areas. Soon a number of people followed and listened to him. The numbers grew daily. Within a short time, his reputation spread. Some people called him a prophet. Others called him a Messiah. And others called him a miracle worker. His followers believed him to be the Son of God. Eventually his followers became known as Christians in the first century.

A more detailed view of Jesus' daily life will provide a clearer picture of him. What type of house did he live in? What foods did he eat? What kind of clothing did he wear? Was he educated? What diseases prevailed? How did he travel? What were the religious practices of his day?

Palestinian housing for the low income people (Jesus' family) was flat-roofed with an external staircase and inner raised platform built of mud and/or wood. The family used the roof like an extra room since there was usually one room in the house. Joseph's carpenter's shop was part of the house on the ground level. Water was kept in a jar outside the house. The ground floor area was divided into two sections: one area for living, the other for the animals. There was no fireplace. The fire was made in a hole in the earth floor. The wealthy homes were constructed with stone and bricks. They had several rooms with a courtyard in the center of the complex, two or three bedrooms, a dining room, a storeroom, and a cooking area.

With regard to food, Jesus' diet varied and included lentils, corn, beans, onions, cucumbers, garlic, herbs, melons, figs, dates, pomegranates, nuts, grapes and cheese. Fish rather than lamb and veal was eaten. His normal drink would have been milk, wine and water.

Jewish men wore long cotton tunics with a leather

belt. In the wintertime, the poor wore over the tunic a light coat made from goat's hair; the rich man's coat would be made from real wool. Because of the heat, men and women wore a turban or a square piece of cloth held on the head by a cord. Women's clothes were very similar to men's, but more colorful. Footwear consisted of a cowhide sole fastened to the ankle by a leather thong passing between the large and second toes. The wealthier people wore leather sandals.

In Jesus' time a girl's education was still primarily in her mother's hands, but every boy went to the school attached to the synagogue when he was six. History, mathematics, reading and a trade were taught. Jesus learned carpentry. Other trades, such as tanning, masonry, shepherding, fishing and farming, were options to young Jewish boys.

The Jewish community was very aware of personal cleanliness and diseases. Many health regulations were laid down in the Book of Leviticus in the Old Testament. Dysentery, cholera, typhoid, dropsy, blindness, various mental illnesses and leprosy afflicted Palestine and neighboring countries. Every Jewish town had either a physician or a surgeon. Often one reads in the New Testament stories about Jesus curing lepers, blindness and mental illness.

How did Jesus travel? Like many ordinary people of the day, he went on foot. There were times when he used donkeys, the chief means of transportation for poor people. Wealthier people traveled by horse, carriages, or chariots. Camels and donkeys were used for those traveling together as a caravan for safety against thieves. We know that Jesus traveled by caravan to Jerusalem when he was twelve years old. There may have been other times as well.

Finally, the religious life of Jesus centered on the prescriptions of the law (torah), annual festivals, the temple, the synagogue and the Sanhedrin. The law laid down regulations governing sacrifice and offering, purification rites and other features. The great day of the year was (and still is) the Day of Atonement, which was observed by fast, abstinence and prayer in atonement for one's sins. The other great festivals were (and still are): Passover, commemorating the escape from Egypt; Tabernacles, held in the autumn when all the fruit crops had been harvested; Purim, celebrating Esther's deliverance of the Jews; Pentecost, commemorating the beginning of harvest. As mentioned before, these observations continue into the present day.

However, the heart of Jewish life was the weekly sabbath service at the synagogues and the temple. Every town, village and city had at least one synagogue building. The synagogue service basically consisted of prayers, Scripture readings from the law (torah) and prophets, a sermon, and a question period. Only men took an active part in the service. Women and children sat in the gallery section. Jesus went regularly to the synagogue (Lk 4:16–30). Like many faithful Jews, Jesus probably attended daily religious services. In regard to the temple, there was only one temple in all of Palestine. By law, every Jewish person was required to make three trips to the temple annually. Illness, financial problems or great distances were excusing circumstances. The temple was one of the wonders of the world. Most noteworthy was its design, furnishings and size. Located in Jerusalem, it rested on thirty-five acres. Every day hundreds of worshipers came for morning and evening services. Besides animal sacrifices, there were prayers, meditations, sermons and discussions. The duties of the priests and Levites were primarily the daily animal sacrifices and worship. The Gospels (Mt 4:11; 27:51; Lk 2:22; 21:1–4; Mk 11:11; Jn 2:20) speak of Jesus' presence at the temple.

The religious life of the synagogues and the temple was controlled by the religious council called the Sanhedrin. This council was the supreme court which resided in Jerusalem. Composed of seventy-one members from elders, lawyers, Pharisees, and Sadducees, their civil and religious jurisdiction extended only to Judea, but Jews everywhere respected the council's authority and were influenced by it.

Titles

During Jesus' time, certain titles either were used by Jesus himself, or were given to him by his followers. The Old Testament literature uses the title "Son of Man" collectively and individually. Many times it means a human individual. The prophet Ezekiel is called the Son of Man approximately ninety times. The Book of Enoch clearly speaks of a pre-existent individual (48:2–3) who will appear at the end of the world and judge it (62:2–4). Yet the passage in the Book of Daniel (7:13) uses the title collectively. It speaks of a human figure representing the "Holy Ones of the Most High." The New Testament frequently uses this title for Jesus. It occurs approximately twenty times in the Synoptic Gospels, twelve times in John's writings and once in the Acts of the Apostles. Paul does not use the term, but speaks of Jesus as "the Man" (Rom 5:12–20) and "the Last Adam" (1 Cor 15:49). From these New Testament texts, Jesus seems to be speaking of an individual. Interestingly, it is the only title Jesus regularly applied to himself.

The "Son of God" title is frequently used by Jesus' followers to denote his divinity with God the Father. Although Jesus never technically used the term himself, he frequently referred to his Sonship with the Father (Mt 11:27; Mk 13:32; Lk 22:29; Jn 1:14; Col 1:13). The New Testament usage of the term occurs eleven times in Matthew, seven times in Mark, nine times in Luke, two times in Acts, seventeen times in John's writings, and eighteen times in Paul's letters. Thus, the evangelists stated clearly the central fact of Jesus' life and person, his divinity, which was implied in his words and actions.

Perhaps Jesus never spoke of himself as the Messiah (the anointed one) because of the various popular Jewish notions circulating during his time. The Pharisees expected a religious-political leader like Moses. The Essenes expected two Messiahs, a religious leader and a military leader. The Zealots expected a revolutionary national leader. In all cases, the Messiah would be a human being, not divine. Gradually, Jesus revealed his notion of the Messiah. He would be the suffering servant who has come to establish God's Kingdom on earth. He is the Messiah who has come to save all peoples and to judge the living and the dead at the end of the world. Jesus' followers eventually came to understand his corrected usage of the Hebrew word Messiah and its Greek equivalent Christos (Christ). In the New Testament, apart from two passages (Jn 1:41; 4:25), the Greek word Christos is used instead of the Hebrew word Messiah.

Closely associated with the title Messiah (Christ) and Son of God was that of Lord. The Hebrew word in the Old Testament signifies several meanings: ruler (3 Kgs 22:17), an owner of slaves (Gn 24:9), a polite greeting (Gn 23:6). Yahweh (God) is called Lord in the Old Testament writings because he created his people and therefore legitimately owned and ruled them (Is 1:24; Ex 119:4; Jos 3:11). In the New Testament, Lord was also used in greeting a superior (Mt 13:27) and as a title of respect for an equal, similar to the English word "Sir" (Jn 12:21). The Gospels of Mark and Matthew refer to Jesus as Lord only once (Mk 11:3; Mt 21:3). Luke uses the term fifteen times. John's Gospel calls Jesus "the Lord" in texts describing post-resurrection events (Jn 20:2, etc.). Jesus is called Lord more than twenty times in Acts, and more than one hundred and thirty times in the Pauline letters (Phil 2:5–11; Rom 1:4; 1 Cor 14:37, etc.). By applying to Jesus the Hebrew term "Lord" which was given to Yahweh in the Old Testament, the New Testament writers were acknowledging the divinity of Jesus. It was the earliest title used by the Christian community after the resurrection of Jesus to designate his divinity.

The Old Testament applied the title Savior hundreds of times to Yahweh (Dt 32:15; Ps 25:5; Is 12:2). The central theme of the Old Testament is salvation. In the New Testament this title is not only given to God (Lk 1:47; 1 Tim 1:1), but even more often to Jesus (Lk 2:10; Jn 4:42; Acts 5:31; Phil 3:20, etc.). From all of these texts, God the Father is the initiator of salvation and Jesus carries out this work of salvation on both a temporal and a spiritual level. Because of the action of God the Father and Jesus, people are delivered from their sins and are given eternal life. Jesus brings to perfection the Old Testament notion of Yahweh as Savior. Jesus is, therefore, "the Savior of the world" (Jn 4:41; 1 Jn 4:14).

Many passages in the Old Testament depict God as communicating with people by means of words (Gn 2:16–17; Jos 3:7–8; Is 6:9–10). In these words, God manifests his saving commands. Although the New Testament writers develop and expand God's words, John's writings only address Jesus with the title "the Word." In the Johannine writings, Jesus is the Word. The clearest expression of this idea is found in his prologue. The prologue of John (1:1–14) identifies Jesus with the Father (1:1), the personal distinction of Jesus from the Father (1:4), Jesus revealing the glory of the Father which he shares (1:14). The main emphasis in John's Gospel is that Jesus and the Father are one (Jn 10:30). Throughout John's writings, therefore, the human Jesus, the Word, is the revelation of his mission, his origin and his deeper nature. Jesus is that pre-existing Son (Jn 1:17–18) or the Word (Jn 1:14) through whom all things are made (Jn 1:1–3).

Finally, three other titles given to Jesus—Master, Teacher and Rabbi—are found several times in Matthew and Mark. Such honorary titles were usually given to Jewish teachers. They did not imply any theological significance. However, the theological title "Son of David" is addressed to Jesus twice in the Synoptic writings: the curing of the blind man (Mk 10:47) and the question about David's son (Mt 22:42). The only other reference is found in Paul's letters (Rom 1:3; 2 Tim 2:8).

Message

Jesus' teaching is concrete, striking and living. At other times his words are paradoxical, hyperbolic and provocative. But always there is the central idea to repent and reform one's life. These ideas are at the core of his key message—the Kingdom of God.

Mark's Gospel summarizes it: "This is the time of fulfillment; the reign of God is at hand. Reform your lives and believe in the Gospel" (1:15). Matthew's Gospel records the same words, but with one difference. Matthew writes "the Kingdom of heaven." He is conforming to a rabbinical custom of replacing the word God with heaven, out of reverence for the word "God."

Several points about the Kingdom of God can be made:

1. It announces the divine action and demands a response from people.

2. The Kingdom is not an earthly kingdom. Jesus said to Pilate, "My Kingdom is not of this world" (Jn 18:36). Obviously, Jesus is speaking of an eternal Kingdom.

3. The Kingdom is a process. It will grow. "The reign of God is like yeast which a woman took and kneaded into three measures of flour. Eventually the whole mass began to rise" (Mt 13:33).

4. The Kingdom lies in the experience of something being precious (Mt 13:44–45) and the most valuable thing you have—you must be prepared to give everything else up for it. "The reign of God is like a buried treasure which a man found in a field. He hid it again, and rejoicing at his find went and sold all he had and bought that field" (Mt 13:44).

5. The Kingdom will embrace everyone—there will be no exceptions. "The spirit of the Lord is upon me: therefore he has anointed me. He has sent me to bring glad tidings to the poor, to proclaim liberty to the captives, recovery of sight to the blind and re-

lease to prisoners, to announce a year of favor from the Lord" (Lk 4:18–19).

6. The Kingdom is already in your midst (Lk 17:20).

7. The Kingdom is promised only to those with a certain outlook and way. The Sermon on the Mount with the Beatitudes makes this clearer (Lk 6:17–19).

8. The Kingdom can be inherited by loving one's neighbor (Mt 5:38–48). In this section Jesus speaks of the old law of retaliation—an eye for an eye—and says now that we must love our enemies and pray for our persecutors.

9. The Kingdom must be accepted as a child would. Did Jesus mean that one was to return to childhood? No, but one must return to the innocence of childhood. Mark says, "I assure you that whoever does not accept the reign of God like a little child shall not take part in it" (Mk 10:15).

10. The Kingdom will make many demands. To the man who told Jesus that he would be his follower but that first he had to bury his father, Jesus replied: "Let the dead bury their dead. Come away and proclaim the Kingdom of God" (Lk 9:57).

There is nothing more precious to Jesus than the Kingdom of God. It is Jesus' central theme when he preaches.

While Jesus proclaimed the Kingdom of God and gave some idea of what it is, he demanded repentance.

He said that we must reform our lives. To reform, one must have a conversion. The Greeks have a word *metanoia,* which literally means a change of mind. There must be a turning away from a way you recognize to be wrong and taking a new direction. Once one has a conversion, one can repent.

This point is made very clearly in some of Jesus' statements. For instance:

1. Mark quotes Jesus as saying, "People who are healthy do not need a doctor; sick people do. I have come to call sinners, not the self-righteous" (Mk 10:17).

2. Jesus rejoiced over conversions. Luke records, "I tell you, there will be more joy in heaven over one repentant sinner than over the ninety-nine righteous people who do not need repentance" (Lk 15:7). Therefore, reformation and repentance remain the key requirements for the Kingdom of God.

As Jesus preached the Kingdom of God message, many people listened and followed him. Among the hundreds of followers, he picked twelve men to be his key leaders. Andrew, John, Simon (Peter), Philip and Nathanael (Bartholomew) were on intimate terms with Jesus before he formally chose the twelve. They first met him at the river Jordan where they were disciples of John the Baptist (Jn 1:35–51). They stayed with him when he made his headquarters at Capernaum (Jn 2:12). Except for Matthew (Levi) who was called by Jesus while sitting at his tax collector's place, it is unknown how the other apostles met Jesus. The names of the twelve apostles are listed once in each of the Synoptic Gospels (Mt 10:2–4; Mk 2:16–19; Lk 6:14–16) and once in Acts (1:13). Judas Iscariot, who betrayed Jesus, was replaced by Matthias (Acts 1:21–26). The apostles received their commission to teach and preach and baptize from Jesus (Mt 28:19–20). Some witnessed Jesus' resurrection (Lk 24:48). They baptized and celebrated the Eucharist (Acts 2:41; 20:7–11). In God's name they forgave sins (Jn 20:23). They were reminded not to be a master, but a servant of their people (Mk 10:42–45). Theirs is a ministry of service (Rom 11:13).

The apostles were predominantly fishermen. Matthew was a tax collector, and for others, like Judas, little or no information exists about their occupations. A brief look into their lives will give us a clear picture why Jesus may have picked them.

The Apostles

Peter, like many contemporaries, used two names, one Hebrew (Simeon—Greek form, Simon), and one Greek (Peter) (Acts 15:14; 2 Pet 1:1; Mk 1:16). Jesus gave Simon his new name, Cephas (Peter) (Mk 3:16; Jn 1:40). Cephas and Peter are different forms of the same name. Peter is the Greek and Cephas is the Aramaic for a rock. More is known about Peter than any of the other apostles because of the very close friendship of Peter and the Gospel writer Mark. Peter was a fisherman from Bethsaida, a town on Lake Tiberias (Lk 5:3). Archaeologists discovered his house at Capernaum (Mk 1:29). Jesus cured his mother-in-law of a fever (Mk 1:29–31). His brother Andrew also joined Jesus' group (Jn 1:42). Peter was the spokesman for the other apostles (Mt 15:15). Mention is also made of his anger (Mk 10:41), his doubts (Mt 14:31), and his triple denial of Jesus (Mk 14:66–72). He performed many cures, among them that of the lame man

(Acts 3:1–4). At the first council meeting in Jerusalem in A.D. 49–50 he presided when it was officially stated that Gentile converts to Christianity were not subject to the Jewish law of circumcision and certain dietary regulations. It was Peter who always asked questions: the fig tree (Mk 11:21), the end of the world (Mk 13:3) and taxes (Mt 17:24). Many biblical scholars agree that Peter was martyred in Rome during the reign of Emperor Nero between A.D. 62–64. Recent archaeological discoveries under St. Peter's Basilica in Rome have unearthed Peter's bones, although some scholars have disputed their authenticity.

Born in Bethsaida, Andrew was a native of Galilee. Like his brother Peter, he lived by the seacoast in Capernaum. He and John the evangelist were disciples of John the Baptist (Jn 1:35–50), but left him to follow Jesus. Andrew urged Peter to follow Jesus (Jn 1:40–42). It was he who introduced a young boy with five loaves and two fishes to Jesus (Jn 6:8–9). One day some Greeks came to Philip to see Jesus. When Philip asked Andrew what to do, it was he who said that they must be brought to Jesus (Jn 12:20–22). With these incidents, information about Andrew in the New Testament comes to an end. Legend and tradition say that he traveled to Cappadocia, Bithynia, Galatia and Asia Minor. It is generally accepted that he was martyred in Patros on the west coast of Greece in A.D. 69. Because of his extensive missionary activity, he is presently the patron saint of Russia, Scotland and Greece.

Although there is little known about Matthew's personal life, there is a lot known about his public life. Matthew's other name was Levi. Both he and his brother were sons of Alphaeus (Mk 2:4). He was a tax collector at Capernaum (Lk 5:27), sometimes called a publican (an officer who collected the Roman taxes). Unlike some of the other apostles, Matthew did not come from John the Baptist's disciples. He is one of the four evangelists who recorded Jesus' ministry. His audience was the Jewish Christian in Palestine. He wrote about Jewish practices, customs and historical traditions which would give insights into Jesus as the promised Messiah. Matthew had perhaps the best education of any of the apostles. His ministry seems to have taken him from Palestine to Persia and perhaps to Ethiopia in Africa. The evidence of his martyrdom in Egypt is historically unreliable. He may have died a normal death.

James the brother of Matthew is the apostle about whom we know very little. The New Testament records his name (Mt 10:3; Mk 3:18; Lk 6:15; Acts 1:13). Since he was the son of Alphaeus, who was a Zealot, it can be reasonably assumed that James also belonged to the Jewish nationalist party (Zealots) (Mt 13:55). Paul mentions him with Peter and John as one of the pillars of the Church (Gal 2:9). At the Council of Jerusalem he favored reconciliation between the Gentile and the Jewish Christians. Stories about his journeys to Constantinople, being a Nazarite, and his physical resemblance to Jesus cannot be historically verified. Tradition says that he died when he was thrown from the walls of the great temple in Jerusalem in A.D. 62.

Like Peter and Andrew, Philip came from Bethsaida. He was one of the first apostles called by Jesus and was instrumental in introducing Nathanael (Bartholomew) to Jesus (Jn 1:43–49). Although the Synoptic writers do not mention any incidents with Philip, John records three occasions. First, Philip asks Jesus where will they buy bread to feed so many people (Jn 6:5–7). Second, several Greeks asked Philip to introduce them to Jesus (Jn 12:20–

22). Third, at the Last Supper, Jesus tells Philip that anyone who sees him (Jesus) sees the Father (Jn 14:8f). Like his apostolic contemporaries, he brought the message of Jesus to many areas of the Roman Empire. Historically, it seems fairly certain that he was martyred in Hierapolis, Turkey when he was very old.

Thomas is the Greek translation of the Aramaic *Toma,* which means twin. The Synoptic Gospels say nothing about him except his name. Practically all the information about him is found in John's Gospel. As a man of courage, Thomas is willing to go with Jesus to Bethany to see Lazarus, despite death threats (Jn 11:16). His skepticism is mentioned after not knowing the way (Jn 14:1–7). Thomas is also mentioned as being present at the miracle of the fishes on Lake Tiberias (Jn 21:1–8). Early Christian literature speaks of his activity in Babylon, Persia, Constantinople and India. Certainly, there is some historical truth to these statements. Likewise, there is historical evidence to support the point that he died and was buried in Mylapore, India, now a suburb of Madras.

Very little is known with certainty of Bartholomew (Nathanael). Again, we see here the family name, Bartholomew (bar-Talmai) and the first name, Nathanael. He came from Galilee, as did most of the apostles. Jesus said beautiful things about him (Jn 1:47–51). John's Gospel speaks of Philip, who brought Nathanael to Jesus (Jn 1:45). Outside of his name being mentioned (Mt 10:3; Mk 3:18; Lk 6:14; Acts 1:13) and this one incident in John's Gospel, there is no other information about him. Most of what we know comes from early Christian writers such as Eusebius and Jerome. Nathanael seems to have preached generally in the area around the south end of the Caspian Sea in the section that was then called Armenia, but which today is divided between Iran and the Soviet Union.

The Zebedee family had two apostles, John and James. John was a fisherman of Galilee. Both he and his brother were partners with Andrew and Peter in the fishing business. Because of their violent tempers, it has been suggested that they were called "sons of thunder" (Mk 3:17; 9:37–40). At the instigation of their mother, they asked for special positions in Jesus' Kingdom (Mt 20:20–23). John witnessed the restoration of life to the daughter of Jairus (Mk 5:37). He was one of the apostles chosen to prepare for the Last Supper (Lk 22:8). At the crucifixion of Jesus, he is present (Jn 19:29f). At the Sea of Tiberias, he was the first to recognize the risen Jesus (Jn 21:1–7). John appears frequently in the Synoptic Gospels, but never once does he appear by name in the Gospel of John. But in John's Gospel there appears a man called the beloved disciple. It has been suggested that it is John the apostle. One cannot say with certainty that this is true. Likewise, it is not certain that John the apostle is the author of the Gospel. John was a very popular name in Jesus' era. Eusebius the historian says that John died and was buried in the city of Ephesus which today is in Turkey.

John's brother James was the first of the apostles to become a martyr. He and Judas are the only apostles about whom we have a scriptual account of their deaths. With John and Peter, he belonged to the inner circle who were with Jesus on the most sacred occasions (Mk 5:37). Like his brother, he was promised by Jesus that they would drink his cup (suffering) (Mk 10:35–40). James was one of the four who questioned Jesus concerning the last things. The Acts of the Apostles (12:1–2) records that he was murdered by King Herod Agrippa I about A.D. 44. The *Encyclopaedia Britannica* says: "There is a tradition open to serious difficulties and not unanimously admitted that James preached the Gospel in Spain and that after his death his body was transported to Compostelia (Spain)" (Vol. 11, p. 120). There does seem to be some historical evidence that some of his bones may have been taken back to Spain where he had once preached.

Simon the Zealot and Simon the Canaanite are one and the same person. The New Testament tells us nothing but his name (Mt 10:4; Mk 3:18; Lk 6:15; Acts 1:13). There has been some speculation that he is the brother of James, son of Alphaeus and Jude. Being a member of the Zealot party, he would have been most nationalistic in his ways. The Zealots were the last of the great Jewish parties to emerge. They were fervent patriots. One is reminded of their final fight at Masada, Herod's fortress on the seashore of the Dead Sea. Early Christian writings place his ministry in North Africa, Greece, Spain and Britain. He is believed to have been martyred in Persia.

Perhaps the strangest apostle had three names. In Mark he is called Thaddaeus (Mk 3:18); in Matthew he is called Lebbaeus, whose surname was Thaddaeus (Mt 10:3); in Luke he is called Judas the brother of James (Lk 6:16; Acts 1:13). The Synoptic Gospels are silent about his activity. John's Gospel mentions the only incident about him. At the Last Supper he asked Jesus the question: "Lord, why is it that you will reveal yourself to us and not to the world?" (14:22). All other information about him comes from early Christian writings such as The Gospel of the Ebionites, Genealogies of the Twelve Apostles, The Book of Bede and others. His years of evangelization seem to have been in Syria and Northern Persia.

The last apostle to be mentioned is Judas Iscariot.

History remembers him as the apostle who betrayed Jesus. Unlike the other apostles who came from Galilee, he came from Carioth, a city of Judea. He carried the purse for the apostles (Jn 12:6). His betrayal is related in all of the Gospels (Mk 14:43–45; Lk 22:47f; Mt 26:47–54; Jn 18:2f). His annoyance at the woman anointing Jesus' feet with very precious ointment is noted especially in John's Gospel (12:1–8). The New Testament closes the Judas story in Acts 1:25 where it is said that Matthias was chosen to replace him after his death. Without further comment, it suffices to say that Judas remains a tragic story.

The Christian Communities

The Palestinian-Jewish community was composed of the Jewish converts from Palestine. They came to understand Jesus in light of their Jewish heritage (laws, prophecies and customs). They were the original converts of the good news (Gospel). The Hellenistic-Jewish community was composed of Jewish converts from areas outside of Palestine. Because of their openness to other cultures, they were more receptive to Jesus' messages. The Gentile community was composed of non-Jews who converted to Christianity. This group was the largest among the Christian converts. They eventually outnumbered the Jewish-Christians in the Church. At times, quarrels arose between these two groups because of their cultural differences.

Summary

1. Jesus was born in Bethlehem (Judea), Palestine c. 4 B.C. and died in Jerusalem c. 30 A.D.

2. Every poor Jewish family had a flat-roofed house with an external staircase and inner raised platform. Jewish diet consisted of lentils, corn, beans, onions, cucumbers, fish, milk, wine, water and so forth. Jewish men wore long cotton tunics with a leather belt. Education consisted of history, mathematics, reading and learning a trade. Diseases such as dysentry, cholera, typhoid, dropsy, blindness, and leprosy afflicted Palestine and neighboring countries. The chief means of transportation was the donkey.

3. The religious life of a Jewish person centered on reading the torah, observance of the festivals, and attendance at the temple and synagogue.

4. The Sanhedrin was the Jewish senate. It consisted of seventy-one men, including the high priest.

5. There was only one temple located in Jerusalem, situated on thirty-five acres of land. There was at least one synagogue in every town and city in Palestine.

6. Various titles were attributed to Jesus: Son of God, Son of Man, Messiah, Christ, Lord, Savior, the Word, Master, Teacher, Rabbi, Son of David. The Son of Man title was the only one used by Jesus of himself.

7. Jesus' central message is the Kingdom of God. Repent and reform are at the core of his message.

8. The Kingdom of God is divine, a process that is precious, embraces everyone, is conditional and demands a change of heart.

9. Jesus' apostles were predominately fishermen. The twelve apostles were Peter, Andrew, Matthew, James, son of Alphaeus, Philip, Thomas, Bartholomew, John and James Zebedee, Simon the Zealot, Thaddaeus and Judas Iscariot.

10. There were three Christian communities: Palestinian-Jewish Christians, Hellenistic-Jewish Christians, and Gentile Christians.

Discussion Questions

1. Briefly state the facts of Jesus' earthly life.

2. Describe the housing and education system during Jesus' time.

3. What was the ordinary diet of an average Jewish person?

4. What is the Day of Atonement, Passover, Tabernacles, Purim and Pentecost?

5. Define: Sanhedrin, temple, synagogue.

6. Briefly explain these titles: Son of Man, Son of God, Messiah, Christ, Lord, Savior, the Word, Master, Teacher, Rabbi and Son of David.

7. What was the earliest title used by the Christian community to describe Jesus?

8. Compare the Old and New Testament usage of the word Savior.

9. Why are John's writings unique?

10. Summarize the Kingdom of God idea.

11. What would exclude one from the Kingdom of God?

12. What is metanoia?

13. List the conditions Jesus laid down for his apostles.

14. Give a brief character sketch of each apostle.

15. Which apostles were not fishermen? Did all apostles come from Galilee? Were there any brothers among the apostles? Who was Nathanael?

16. Why were the Zebedee brothers called "sons of thunder"? Who became the first martyr among the apostles? Which apostle is called by three names in the New Testament?

17. Define: Palestinian-Jewish Christians, Hellenistic-Jewish Christians, Gentile Christians.

Suggested Reading

Pat Alexander, ed., *The Lion Concise Bible Encyclopedia.* England: Lion Publishing, 1980.
William Barclay, *The Master's Men.* Nashville: Abingdon, 1959.

William McBirnie, *The Search for the Twelve Apostles.*
    Wheaton: Tyndale House Publishers, 1973.
Albert Rouet, *A Short Dictionary of the New Testament.*
    New York/Ramsey: Paulist Press, 1982.
John Steinmuller and Kathryn Sullivan, *Catholic Biblical
    Encyclopedia.* New York: Joseph F. Wagner, Inc.,
    1956.

3

The New Testament Writings' Portrait of Jesus

The New Testament Writings

Two thousand years ago Jesus of Nazareth walked the streets of the various towns and cities of Palestine (Israel today). As the Gospels tell us, he discussed and debated with the Pharisees, Sadducees, Herodians, high priests and scribes. His favorite topic was the Kingdom of God. Crowds followed him: some curious, some grateful, some hopeful and some disillusioned. We hear of rebels, riots, executions and heavy taxation. Galileans were considered noisy, commercial and cosmopolitan. Samaritans were hated and avoided. Judeans were conservative. Unlike the prophets of the Old Testament, Jesus mingled with sinners, publicans, tax collectors, prostitutes, lawyers and lepers.

Once Jesus died, the new community of believers shared his mission. The Acts of the Apostles depicts the emergence of Christianity from its Jewish roots into a religion of worldwide status. Stage by stage it relates the importance of Jerusalem as the mother church, the seat of the twelve apostles, and the doctrinal focal point of Christian missionary activity, namely the work of the Holy Spirit. The first section of the book speaks of the first Christian community in Palestine. The second part covers the missionary journeys of Paul who brought Christianity to Asia Minor and Rome.

The Book of Revelation is the most difficult New Testament writing to understand because of its apocalyptic and prophetic images. The Book of Revelation (the Apocalypse) is the cry of the persecuted and oppressed Christians in the first century. The author, John, calls upon the followers of Christ to give witness and be prepared to suffer the consequences even unto martyrdom. The power of God will overcome the forces of evil. The good will be rewarded. The wicked will be punished.

Finally, there are the letters of Paul, James, Peter, John and Jude. Paul's thirteen letters were addressed to individual churches and individuals. Their basic purpose was to answer questions about the faith and discipline problems and to clear up misunderstandings. The Letter to the Hebrews speaks of the superiority of Jesus to persecuted Jewish Christians. The other letters are general in nature and were addressed to a wider group than local churches or individuals.

Briefly that is the picture of the New Testament writings. But questions are asked: how did these writings come into existence? Who wrote them? When were they written? Why were they written?

The Gospels

The English word gospel comes from the Anglo-Saxon terms *god* (good) and *spell* (tale). This word translates the Greek word *evangelion*. From this Greek word we get the word "evangelist" which means "one who proclaims the good news." The Gospel is not merely a recitation or an announcement. It commits the listener to the teachings of Jesus. Today the Gospels are generally viewed as biographies of Jesus. They do give various details of his life and ideas. Yet they are not really biographies. They are statements of faith about human beings and the world and God's relation to each person.

The four Gospels (Matthew, Mark, Luke, John) have the general aim of arousing and strengthening the faith of Christians. Each one has a distinctive theme or themes. Matthew's Gospel emphasizes the role of community. Mark's Gospel urges the call to discipleship. Luke's Gospel speaks of God's care for the poor and lowly. John's Gospel portrays Jesus as the light among us now.

The first three Gospels (Matthew, Mark, Luke) are called Synoptic because they report many of the same happenings and sayings of Jesus' life. Yet there are significant differences in content and form. But Matthew, Mark and Luke stand much closer to each other than any one of them does to John. John does not repeat many points found in the Synoptic Gospels. In contrast with the Synoptics, John's Gospel is a Gospel of the person of Jesus himself. Jesus is the pre-existent Son and Word in whom God the Father is revealed.

Before we examine each Gospel, we will analyze how they came into existence. Biblical scholars generally agree that there are three levels of development.

The First Level: The sayings and actions of Jesus existed long before the written accounts. Jesus in his lifetime preached and taught in the various towns and cities in Palestine. The watchword of Jesus' message was re-

pentance. If one repents, one would reform. Then the
Kingdom of God would be accomplished. He called the
disciples who were fishermen to be fishers of men and
women. He spoke to farmers in terms of grain sown and
harvested, to vintagers in terms of vineyards and grapes,
to landowners in terms of slaves and servants. He criticized the hypocrisy of certain Pharisees and Sadducees.
He comforted the afflicted like the widow of Naim. He
cured the lepers. His moral advice is summed up in the
Sermon on the Mount. His message was to all who were
ready to receive it—tax collectors, prostitutes, Jews, non-
Jews, rich and poor.

The Second Level: These stories about Jesus circulated throughout Palestine during his lifetime and after
his death. Approximately from A.D. 30–60, the community of believers used the sayings and actions in accordance with its various functions, needs and interests. They
proclaimed all these things to fellow Christians and po-
tential converts. After the initial proclamation (*kerygma*)
was heard and accepted, the new Christians would desire
to know more about Jesus and the religious implications
of his teachings. The early Christian teachers naturally
adopted various ways of communicating these ideas.
Technically this is called the *Didache* (instructions). They
existed in various forms: catechisms, narratives, testimonies, hymns, prayers, etc. No doubt the apostles and
eyewitnesses to Jesus' sayings and actions exercised a
strict control on what was taught. They would have been
very mindful of handing on exactly what Jesus did and
said lest some confusion might arise among the members.

The Third Level: Approximately from A.D. 60–100, the
written accounts of the Gospels appear. The Gospel writ-

ers (evangelists) made use of available printed material and verifiable oral material. All four evangelists have the same general structure: (1) the baptism of Jesus; (2) the ministry in Galilee; (3) the final journey to Jerusalem; (4) the passion, death and resurrection of Jesus. Apart from this general structure, the evangelists vary in their arrangement of the material. The reason is simple. Matthew, who was an apostle of Jesus, wrote for a Jewish-Christian audience. His main theme was to show that Jesus was the expected Messiah promised to the Jews. Mark, a disciple of Peter, appealed to the Roman Christians. His emphasis was placed on the titles of Jesus, the Christ and Son of Man. Paul's convert, Luke, urged his Gentile-Christian congregation to appreciate Jesus' identification with the poor, outcasts and so forth. Finally, John, whether he be the apostle or a disciple of Jesus, reached out to all peoples. For him, Jesus is the Messiah, superior to all prophets including John the Baptist. Obviously the four evangelists give four different portraits of Jesus. They are not concerned about a biography of Jesus. As a result, we do not have the exact date of his birth and death, the length of the public ministry, the number of times he traveled to Jerusalem, or the exact order of events in his last week. Each wrote according to his personal character and with a special aim for special needs. Apparently, each Gospel circulated individually at first, until the beginning of the second century when the four were put together.

We have examined how the Gospels came into existence. We will now turn our attention to the three other questions: Who wrote them? When were they written? Why were they written?

The Gospel of Mark

Mark, the missionary companion of Paul and disciple of Peter, wrote his Gospel between A.D. 65–70. His full name was John Mark (Acts 12:12–25). He was a Jew from the Greek-speaking world, the son of a woman converted to Christianity (Acts 12:12) and a cousin of Barnabas (Col 4:10). It is generally believed that he wrote the Gospel in Rome for Roman Christians.

Mark's Gospel has been called the Gospel of action because he emphasizes Jesus' actions more than words. Mark records the feeding of the five thousand (6:39), healing of the withered hand (3:5), the calming of the storm (4:38), the healing of Jairus' daughter (5:41), the blessing of the children who came to him (10:16), and the rich young man who came to see Jesus (10:21). These actions of Jesus would comfort the hundreds of Christians suffering the persecution of the Roman Emperor Nero. Mark's message is clear: the followers of Jesus must be prepared to suffer as Jesus himself suffered. Finally, *Mark's main theme is: Jesus is the Messiah, the Son of God and the Son of Man.*

Except for fifty verses, Mark's gospel is contained either in Matthew or in Luke or in both of these Gospels. Peculiar to Mark are two miracles (the cure of the deaf mute and the blind man at Bethsaida), one parable (the seed that grows steadily from its own power), and two situations (the large crowd in the house where Jesus was preaching and the naked flight of the young man at Gethsemani).

The Gospel of Matthew

The apostle Matthew was a tax collector. In Mark's Gospel we read that Matthew's other name was Levi. There is nothing odd about a man in his time having two names. Probably he changed his name from Levi to Matthew after his conversion to Jesus. Most likely he did not want to be remembered as the tax-collector Levi who would have been hated by his fellow Jews. He was a Greek-speaking Jew who wrote for the Jewish Christians. His Gospel was written sometime between A.D. 80–90 in Palestine. Some people have called Matthew's Gospel the "Jewish Gospel." It is evident that he was a Jew writing to fellow Jews. The following facts make that clear: (1) the numerous Old Testament references, (2) the emphasis upon the kingship (messiahship) of Jesus, (3) the emphasis of Jesus' mission to the lost sheep of Israel.

His audience (Jewish Christians living in Palestine) had two practical problems: (1) they were struggling against their fellow Jews who accused them of infidelity to God; (2) they were struggling with Gentile (non-Jews) converts who refused to submit to Jewish traditions.

Matthew's central theme is the Kingdom of God. Many Christians held two different views concerning the coming of the Kingdom of God. Some held that it was strictly a future event. It would be established at the end of the age but not until after the earthly kingdoms were destroyed. Others held that the Kingdom was already present. Matthew's Gospel supports both theories. Perhaps Matthew believed that the Kingdom here and now is a preparation for a more complete establishment at some future time. Matthew generally avoids the term "Kingdom of God" in favor of the term "Kingdom of Heaven" because of the Jewish reverence for the sacred name of

God. His Gospel is not only the Gospel of the Kingdom but the Gospel of the Church. Matthew's Gospel is the only one to use the word "Church" (18:17; 16:18). Matthew sees the Church as the continuance of the covenant people.

The Gospel of Luke

According to ancient traditions, Luke was a physician and sometime traveling companion of Paul. Actually, he is the author of a Gospel and another New Testament writing called the Acts of the Apostles. While Matthew's Gospel has been called the "Jewish Gospel," Luke's Gospel has been called the "Gentile Gospel." Naturally, both assertions are not completely correct. Like Matthew, Luke also appeals to other groups. However, Luke's primary audience was the Gentile Christian community in Asia Minor. Probably written anywhere from A.D. 70 to 85, his Gospel seems to avoid matters with which Gentiles might not be familiar. For example, he eliminates references to the Jewish temple, services, Jewish names, Jewish laws and customs. It is the only Gospel addressed to a particular person. In ancient times, it was customary to dedicate a work to some famous person to insure its wider circulation. In this case, Luke dedicates his work to Theophilus, probably a Roman official. *Luke's main purpose is that Jesus is the Savior of all people, not just the Jews.* He is the friend of the poor, the rich, the outcast, sinners and women. In Luke, the importance of women and Jesus' concern for them is heavily stressed. For example, the word "woman" occurs forty-three times. Women like Elizabeth, Mary, Anna, the woman prostitute, the widow of Naim, Martha and others are mentioned. Finally, Luke speaks of the joy of salvation which Jesus brought to the world.

The Gospel of John

In the three other Gospels we learn what Jesus was, and John presents the completion of who Jesus was. While the other three writers are concerned about Jesus' public statements, John emphasizes Jesus' private conversations and thoughts. For John, Jesus is the God-Man. But who is the author John? Several theories prevail. Tradition says that he was John, the son of Zebedee, the beloved disciple (apostle) of Jesus. He came from a wealthy family, and knew the high priest personally. Some scholars disagree. They believe he was a disciple of John the apostle. Today, however, there is general agreement that the Gospel was put together in its final form by the disciple John. However, this disciple would have gotten his material basically from John the apostle. John's Gospel was written between A.D. 90 and 100, probably in the city of Ephesus (today, Turkey). There is no doubt that this Gospel was intended not for a specific culture group, but for the world. The key verse is, "For God so loved the world that he gave his only Son, that whoever believes in him should not perish but have eternal life." In other words, *John's main purpose is to show that Jesus is the light for every human being both present and future.* The other themes are life, love, truth and the Father-Son relationship.

The following stories are found only in John and not in the Synoptic Gospels: (1) the wedding feast at Cana

(2:1–11), (2) the story of Nicodemus (3:1–21), (3) the Samaritan woman (4:1–42), (4) the healing at the pool of Bethsaida (5:1–9), (5) the raising of Lazarus (11:1–44), and (6) the washing of the apostles' feet (13:1–20).

Finally, it is not the similarities but the differences that are striking between John and the other three Gospels (the Synoptics). Ninety percent of John's Gospel is different from the other Gospels. The differences are extensive. In John there is no baptism scene, no demon exorcisms, no parables. The Synoptic writers and John differ on the length of Jesus' ministry. John mentions that Jesus celebrated three Passovers. The Synoptics record one Passover scene. Whether or not John knew the Synoptic Gospels, it is certain that he did not use them as source material for his own writing.

The Synoptic Problem

The Synoptic problem arises from the contents of Matthew, Mark and Luke's Gospels. If the contents of these Gospels are placed in parallel columns, section by section, certain remarkable resemblances and divergences appear. These similarities and dissimilarities may be recognized in (1) the subject matter, (2) the arrangement of the subject matter, and (3) the mode of expression.

The Gospel of Mark is the shortest of the three Synoptic writings, containing only about fifty verses peculiar to Mark. Almost the whole of Mark is found also in Matthew or Luke or both. Half of the verses in Matthew's Gospel are peculiar to it. The Gospel of Luke has a little more than half of Mark's material. The Gospels of Matthew and Luke share a considerable amount of material which does not appear in Mark.

Where are their similarities? On the whole, all three Gospels report the same content (words and deeds of Jesus). The miracles, parables, discussions and main events in his life are the same. All three Gospels essentially follow the same arrangement: John the Baptist's preaching, the baptism of Jesus, Jesus' temptations, the ministry of Jesus in Galilee, his journey to Jerusalem, and the events of Jesus' last days.

Finally, the language (wording) is identical or almost identical. There are sections where whole sentences or groups of sentences correspond word for word. For example, Mark's (6:1–6) and Luke's (4:14–30) accounts of Jesus being rejected at Nazareth and Mark's (3:13–19) and Luke's (6:12–16) accounts of the call of the apostles illustrate this point.

The dissimilarities occur also in the content arrangement and language. For example, Matthew's account of the Our Father has seven petitions, but in Luke it has only five, and to some extent the two records differ in wording. Mark and Luke speak of the cure of one possessed man at Gadara, one blind man at Jericho, and one animal at the entrance of Jesus into Jerusalem. In all these cases, Matthew speaks of two posessed men, two blind men and two animals. For another example, Matthew and Luke give the history of Jesus' infancy, whereas Mark does not. As far as language (wording) is concerned, Matthew and Luke are either very similar or virtually identical, but Mark shares no parallels with them.

Although Luke and Matthew share many of Jesus' sayings not found in Mark, they arrange these sayings differently. In Matthew, the sayings are grouped in five major discourses of Jesus, whereas in Luke much of this material is spread throughout Jesus' long journey to Jerusalem. As far as language is concerned, Matthew and Luke are either very similar or virtually identical, but Mark's wording is very different.

How is this similarity and and dissimilarity to be accounted for? This is the Synoptic problem about which there has been much discussion among Biblical scholars. Below in brief are outlines of possible explanations.

First, the *oral tradition theory* says that all three evangelists got their material from people who committed to memory what they saw or had heard. Either they passed this material on by word of mouth or in some written form. Thus, writing independently of one another, each Synoptic writer has written his account. This explanation explains the differences, but not the similarity of arrangement and language. Second, the *pamphlet theory* proposes that some Christians in various cities wrote down a few of Jesus' sayings and deeds. Some may have written down the parables, others the miracles. This idea helps to explain the blocks of material that are similar but does not explain satisfactorily the kinds of agreements. Third, there is the theory that a *primitive catechism* existed. Matthew and Mark drew from this book. Then the original (Aramaic copy) Matthew was translated into Greek, and this copy was incorporated into Mark, and then Luke drew from Mark's document. Again, there are too many flaws in this theory. Fourth, the *mutual independence theory* states that one Gospel writer simply copied from another. One main problem here is that all important material would have been recorded in each Gospel, which it is not. Fifth, the *document theory* has several variations. The simplest form of this theory is that there were two source documents originally, namely, Mark and an unknown document. Therefore, Matthew and Mark would have drawn from these documents. The problem with this theory is that it does not take into account oral tradition. The Gospels could not have arisen solely as a writing process. The more complex form of this theory is that there were several documents in existence other than Mark's account—for example, a document with just parables of Jesus maybe in Jerusalem, a pamphlet with Jesus' moral sayings in Antioch, a collection of Jesus' cures in Caesarea. Eventually, the Synoptic writers would have drawn from these documents. While it is a very complex possible solution to the Synoptic problem, it is currently the best solution. However, there are difficulties with this solution, such as the thought that Matthew, Mark and Luke may have known one another and could have met on several occasions and shared their material.

There is no satisfactory explanation to the Synoptic problem. Each theory offers some reasonable explanation. It should not disturb us since it is basically a technical biblical problem. What is important is that these men transmitted the basic story of Jesus. Whether Jesus cured two men or one on the road to Jericho is not important. What is important is that he performed cures.

We can conclude the following from these theories on the Synoptic problem: (1) all three Gospels were not composed from a common source; (2) Luke and Matthew copied partly from Mark; (3) Matthew and Mark may have copied from each other; (4) the writer was not always concerned about the exact words of Jesus; (5) Mark's Gospel is the earliest writing; (6) no one theory gives a satisfactory solution; (7) in solving the problem, oral tradition must be considered an important point in the final solution.

The Acts of the Apostles

The traditional title, The Acts of the Apostles, was designated hundreds of years after its composition. The title is misleading because it does not record the actions of all the apostles. In reality, it speaks primarily of Peter and Paul. Acts cannot strictly be called the first Church history, but rather a historical monograph of the first years of Christianity.

Unquestionably, Luke the author of the Gospel is also the author of Acts. As in the Gospel of Luke, there is in Acts the same interest in children, women, the sick, the poor, the rich and the Gentile Christians.

The Acts of the Apostles was probably written between A.D. 61 and 64. The last event of Acts is Paul's imprisonment at Rome (ca. 60–61). Paul was executed by the Emperor Nero at Rome in 64.

Luke wrote for the Gentile Christians primarily. His main purpose is clear: "But you shall receive power when the Holy Spirit has come upon you; and you shall be my (Jesus') witness in Jerusalem and in all Judea and Samaria and to the end of the earth"(1:8).

The book is divided into two parts: the first half (chapters 1–12) dealing with Peter, and the second part (chapters 13–28) with the activity of Paul. While this book is concerned with their actions, it is primarily concerned with the foundation, development and experiences of the primitive Church. The story is grouped around the figures of the two leading apostles: the history of the Christian community among the Jews in Jerusalem and Palestine under the leadership of Peter, and the history of the spread of Christianity over the Greco-Roman world under the leadership of Paul.

A brief outline of the book will illustrate Luke's purpose: (1) the election of Matthias to replace Judas the be-
trayer of Jesus; (2) the establishment of the first Christian
community at Jerusalem; (3) the selection of the first deacons; (4) the martyrdom of Stephen; (5) the missionary
activity of Philip in Samaria and the seacoast cities; (6) the
conversion of Saul (Paul); (7) Herod's persecution in Palestine, the death of James the apostle, and Peter's imprisonment; (8) Paul's first missionary trip and the first
general council of Christians; (9) the second missionary
trip of Paul; (10) the third missionary journey of Paul to
Asia and Europe; (11) Paul's imprisonment in Rome. And
so ends Luke's account. It ends abruptly, and several rea-
sons have been offered: (1) because that is when it was
written; (2) because Luke intended to write another vol-
ume; (3) because the concluding section was lost
through the succeeding ages. No one ever will really
know.

The Book of Revelation (The Apocalypse)

Another New Testament writing is the Book of Revelation. Known as "The Revelation of John," there has
been speculation on the author. Most scholars think it is
either John the apostle or a disciple of John. In either
case, it is written around A.D. 90–95.

It was a terrible time for the Christians. The Roman
Emperor Domitian (A.D. 81–96) declared himself a god
and so he required his subjects to worship him as divine. To John this was blasphemy since one worshiped
God alone. He calls upon Christians to give their witness
to Jesus, to keep themselves clean from the world, and to
be prepared to face martyrdom. His main purpose is to

write a book of consolation for those like himself suffering persecution for the faith and to encourage them to persevere to the end. For the Kingdom of God will be their reward. Other themes emerge such as that good will overcome evil eventually and the evil ones will be punished by God.

The outline of the book is clear, but not its interpretation. Apart from its prologue and epilogue, it consists of seven major sections: (1) the seven letters to the seven churches of Asia Minor (Ephesus, Smyrna, Pergamum, Thystira, Sardis, Philadelphia, and Laodicea); (2) the seven seals (disasters); (3) the seven trumpets (terror); (4) the seven signs; (5) the seven bowls (plagues); (6) the fall of Babylon which represents Rome; (7) the consummation (the final conflict), with Satan cast into hell, a general resurrection, and a final judgment.

To understand the Book of Revelation takes much time and patience. The author is writing to persecuted Christians and is using a code. The purpose of the code is to protect the Christians since this type of literature was banned by the Roman government. Some pieces of the code have been deciphered: for example, the woman represents Israel; the child is the Church; the dragon represents Satan (the devil); the two beasts are Nero and Domitian; the lamb is Jesus. As far as the numbers are concerned, we have a far more difficult task of interpretation. In ancient times, numbers represented more than just a strict arithmetical sense. They conveyed a symbolism. The number 7 conveyed a sense of universal completion; 4 meant the four quarters of the world; 40 indicated the length of a generation; 10 meant a fairly large amount. Two groups of numbers have plagued the biblical scholars for years, namely 666 and 144,000. The best thoughts on the subject hold that 666 is a cryptogram standing for the name of a certain great power, more likely the Emperor Nero. The number 144,000 indicates the heavenly Church in its completion (this 12, the number of the tribes of Israel, multiplied by itself and then multiplied by 1,000, signifying immensity; the 144,000 indicates the fullness of Israel and now the Church is the new Israel). A final note to understanding this book is that it is an attempt to strengthen the Christian faith in times of persecution. Of primary importance in understanding this book is to recognize the apocalyptic and prophetic literary style to which it belongs.

Paul's Letters

Paul was probably the greatest missionary the Christian Church has known. He journeyed through much of the vast Roman Empire, planting the seeds of Christian thought. The date of his birth is uncertain, but it is generally placed between A.D. 5 and 10 at Tarsus in Cilicia (Asia Minor). Born of Jewish parents, he was well educated in Jewish and non-Jewish studies. Like many Jewish children living outside Palestine, Saul (his Jewish name) was given a second name (Paul). Paul is the name by which he is best remembered. Because of his father's status with the Roman government, he enjoyed the privileges of Roman citizenship. He was bilingual (Hebrew-Aramaic and Greek). He studied under the great Jewish rabbi, Gamaliel the Elder and eventually became an ardent Pharisee. Because of his zealousness for the strict observance of Jewish law and traditions, he became a persecutor of Jewish Christians. After some years, he experienced a conversion in Damascus. He became a Christian. From Damascus he went to Jerusalem where he was

at first received coldly by the Christians. Barnabas be-
friended him and introduced him to the apostles. After a
short stay, Paul went back to Cilicia and northern Syria
where he established many Christian communities.

In the Acts of the Apostles an account is given of
Paul's three missionary trips. This account is at times very
detailed, while at other times it is sketchy. Each of the
three journeys begins and, except for the tragic ending of
the third, ends at the city of Antioch. In each city and
town that he evangelizes, Paul first addresses himself to
his fellow Jews. Very few Jews converted to this faith.
Paul's success was with the Gentiles (non-Jews). Thousands converted.

A brief review of his missionary trips will give us a
deeper appreciation of the man called Paul. The *first missionary journey* (A.D. 45–49) brought Paul and Barnabas
to Cyprus, Perga and Antioch in Pisidia. New Christian
communities were also formed in the town Derba. John
Mark was with them until he lost heart. Generally they
were well received, except for an incident when Paul was
beaten and dragged out of the town and left for dead. All
together, Paul and Barnabas covered about 1,400 miles—
most impressive when you consider the rough roads and
slow methods of transportation at the time. The *second
missionary journey* (A.D. 50–53) took three years and covered 2,800 miles. During this journey, Paul took Silas (Barnabas' nephew) and eventually met Timothy who joined
them. Christian communities were formed in Philippi,
Thessalonica, Athens and Corinth. Paul remained for
eighteen months in Corinth where there was great im-
morality. His *third missionary journey* (A.D. 54–57)
brought him to the famous city of Ephesus, after he
passed through the Galatian area and Phrygia. Ephesus
was a large metropolitan city with about a half million

people. Paul's three years in Ephesus were perhaps the most successful of his entire career. Paul would write from Ephesus that here "a door has been opened to me, great and evident" (1 Cor 16:9) through his efforts and those of his companions. His final trip (some call it his fourth missionary journey—A.D. 61–63) to Rome was his last one. During his stay in Rome no restrictions were placed on him while he was under arrest. He could receive visitors and preach. He was acquitted of the charges against him. It is believed that he left Rome and came back to Asia Minor. Eventually, he was rearrested and brought back to Rome. He was beheaded at Rome in A.D. 64 in the reign of Emperor Nero.

Besides his journeys, Paul's unsurpassed zeal for the Christian faith is seen in his letters. At times they were written to church communities. A few were written to individuals. They were generally written to correct misunderstandings and to answer questions about the faith. All were written between A.D. 51–63. At least thirteen letters have survived. Many others have not. While there are different themes in the various letters, one central theme runs throughout all his letters, namely that Christians have a new life because of their commitment to Jesus. A quick glance at his letters will give us an appreciation of Paul's thoughts.

The *main themes of Paul's letters* are:

1. The Letter to the Romans (A.D. 57–58) stresses the relationship between Judaism and Christianity.

2. The First Letter to the Corinthians (A.D. 57) gives advice to the Corinthians on chastity and marriage.

3. The Second Letter to the Corinthians (A.D. 57) urges financial support for the suffering Jewish Christians in Jerusalem.

4. The Letter to the Galatians (A.D. 54–55) speaks of his concern about Galatian Christians backsliding to strict Jewish laws.

5. The Letter to the Ephesians (A.D. 62) discusses the mystery of salvation and the mystery of the Church.

6. The Letter to the Philippians (A.D. 62) warns against false teachings.

7. The Letter to the Colossians (A.D. 62) emphasizes that Christ is the main path to salvation.

8. The First Letter to the Thessalonians (A.D. 51) tells of Christ's second coming.

9. The Second Letter to the Thessalonians (A.D. 52) warns about the imminent second coming of Christ.

10. The First Letter to Timothy (A.D. 63) gives advice to Timothy about handling wrong ideas of some Ephesians.

11. The Second Letter to Timothy (A.D. 63) asks Timothy to protect his community against false teachings.

12. The Letter to Titus (A.D. 62) offers advice to Titus to help Christianize the area.

13. The Letter to Philemon (A.D. 62) asks him to be merciful to his runaway slave Onesimus.

In conclusion, it is fitting to quote from Paul's Letter to the Philippians: "I do not claim that I have already succeeded or have already become perfect. I keep striving to win the prize for which Christ Jesus has already won me to himself. Of course, my brothers, I really do not think that I have already won it; the one thing I do know, however, is to forget what is behind me and do my best to reach what is ahead. So I run straight toward the goal in order to win the prize which is God's call through Christ Jesus to the life above" (3:12–16). It explains his tremendous zeal for the Christian faith.

Other Christian Letters

After the death of the apostles, the Christian faith spread to various parts of the world. Because the problems with which they were concerned were not confined to any one local community, they were written for the general membership of the Church. As far as the authorship of these letters, there are various scholarly opinions. Some believe that they were written by the person to whom they are attributed. Others believe that the authors are anonymous, but that in later years they were attributed to prominent individuals of the Christian movement. This custom was not uncommon in the ancient world. Included in this group of writings are one letter of James, two of Peter, three of John and one of Jude. Finally, a Letter to the Hebrews, author unknown, was written to Jewish Christians stressing the superiority of Christ.

The *Letter of James* (A.D. 60's) states that faith must be accompanied by good works. The discussion of faith and works (2:14–26) caused Martin Luther to consider it very unimportant.

The *First Letter of Peter* (A.D. 60's) was written from Rome to the Christian churches in Asia Minor. It teaches the value of suffering, and it is a "sermon" on the importance of the sacrament of baptism.

The *Second Letter of Peter* (A.D. 100–110) warns against false teachers. In particular, "Peter" reminds his people that the parousia (the second coming of Jesus) will come.

The *Letter of Jude* (A.D. 90's) is an exhortation against a group of heretics within the Church who are creating problems. The most interesting features of this letter are the characteristics of an institutional Church.

The *First Letter of John* (A.D. 100–110) was written by either John the Elder or his disciple. It speaks against the Gnostic heresy which believed that the physical world was inherently evil. It condemns the Docetist heresy which denied the reality of Jesus' body.

The *Second Letter of John* (A.D. 100–110), written by John the Elder or his disciple, is a particular letter addressed to a specific Christian community. It warns the Church against docetism. It also indicates that the Christian Church is a definite and separate group in the world.

The *Third Letter of John* (A.D. 100–110) was written by the same author of the first two letters. It condemns the man Diotrephes who is challenging the authority of the lawful authority of the Church (probably John the Elder). It also urges hospitality to other Christian communities.

The *Letter to the Hebrews* (A.D. late 60's) was probably written by a disciple of Paul. It is basically a sermon rather than a letter. It is directed to believers who are in need of exhortation, guidance and comfort.

In conclusion to this survey of New Testament literature, several points should be made: (1) no single body of literature has influenced the course of Western civilization more than the New Testament; (2) individual pieces of the New Testament literature have been written from many different angles; (3) by the end of the first century, practically all of the New Testament writings were written; (4) the chief source of information about Jesus and his followers come from this material; (5) the Gospels reflect the oral traditions about Jesus' sayings and deeds; (6) the Acts of the Apostles gives a brief history of the early Church covering about thirty years after the death of Jesus; (7) the Book of Revelation is the most difficult literature to understand because of its apocalyptic and prophetic images; (8) the letters of Paul which constitute one-third of the New Testament literature were written before the Gospels; (9) the letters of Paul, James, Peter, Jude and John reflect the growing pains and joys of a small group of believers who became known as Christians.

Summary

1. The New Testament writings are the Gospels, the Acts of the Apostles, the Book of Revelation and the letters of Paul, James, Peter, John and Jude.

2. All New Testament writings were basically written between A.D. 50–100.

3. The Gospels are not biographies, but portraits of Jesus.

4. Matthew, Mark and Luke are called Synoptic Gospels because they report many of the same happenings and sayings of Jesus.

5. Before the Gospels were written, there existed the oral tradition about Jesus and then some other forms of writing such as catechisms, narratives, testimonies, hymns, and prayers.

6. The Gospel writers are called evangelists, meaning the ones who proclaim the good news.

7. Mark's Gospel (A.D. 65–70) is called the Gospel of action because it records the deeds more than the sayings of Jesus. Primarily written for Gentiles.

8. The Gospel of Matthew (A.D. 80–90) emphasizes the kingship (messiahship) of Jesus. Primarily written for Jews.

9. The Gospel of Luke (A.D. 70–85) speaks of Jesus as the Savior of all peoples. It is the only Gospel which stresses Jesus' concern for women. Primarily written for the Gentiles.

10. The Gospel of John (A.D. 90–100) is very different in content from the other Gospels. His main purpose is to show that Jesus is the light for every human being. Primarily written for Jew and non-Jew.

11. The Synoptic problem arises from the contents of Matthew, Mark and Luke's Gospels. How can there be similarities and dissimilarities among them?

12. Possible solutions for the Synoptic problem are: the oral tradition, the pamphlet theory, the primitive catechism theory, the mutual independence theory and the document theory.

13. There is no satisfactory explanation to the Synoptic problem. However, the oral tradition theory is an important point in its final solution.

14. The Acts of the Apostles (A.D. 61–64) was written by Luke. It is primarily concerned with the foundation, development and experiences of the primitive Church.

15. The Book of Revelation (A.D. 90–95) was written either by John the apostle or his disciple. It is also known as "the Apocalypse." Primarily written to encourage persecuted Christians to endure their sufferings and be prepared to suffer martyrdom.

16. The Book of Revelation is a code book which uses many symbols to illustrate various ideas.

17. Paul (Saul) was born at Tarsus in Cilicia and died at Rome (A.D. 5/10–64). Born of Jewish parents, he was well educated in Jewish and non-Jewish studies. He was converted to Christianity at Damascus.

18. Paul's three missionary journeys: first trip (A.D. 45–49) covered Cyprus, Perga and Antioch in Pisidia; second trip (A.D. 50–53) went to Philippi, Thessalonica, Athens and Corinth; third trip (A.D. 54–57) basically went to Galatia, Phrygia and Ephesus.

19. Paul's letters were written between A.D. 51 and 63 to Christian communities and individuals.

20. Paul's letters were written to the Romans, Corinthians, Galatians, Ephesians, Philippians, Colossians, Thessalonians, Timothy, Titus and Philemon.

21. The letters of James, Peter, Jude and John are general letters to the general membership of the Church.

22. The Letter to the Hebrews is addressed to believers in order to encourage and comfort them.

Questions for Discussion

1. Name the different pieces of the New Testament literature.

2. What does the word "Gospel" mean?

3. Which Gospels are considered the Synoptic Gospels? Why?

4. Why is John's Gospel different from the others?

5. Briefly explain the three levels of development behind the written Gospels.

6. Who are the evangelists?

7. Who wrote the Gospels? When were they written? Why were they written?

8. Which Gospel is called the "Gospel of action"? Why?

9. Why did Matthew have two names?

10. What is the central theme of Matthew's Gospel?

11. Which Gospel actually uses the word "Church"?

12. What is the key verse in John's Gospel?

13. Discuss John's idea that Jesus is a light to all human beings.

14. What is the Synoptic problem? What are the possible solutions?

15. Who is the author of the Acts of the Apostles? What is the Acts of the Apostles?

16. Briefly summarize the Acts of the Apostles.

17. Does the Book of Revelation have another name? Why?

18. What is the central message of the Book of Revelation?

19. Explain the problem of numbers in the Book of Revelation. Give examples.

20. Give a brief summary of Paul's life.

21. Outline Paul's three missionary journeys.

22. Mention five letters of Paul and their main themes.

23. What are the other Christian letters? What are their central themes?

24. What are your personal thoughts on the New Testament literature?

Suggested Reading

R. Brown, J. Fitzmyer, and R. Murphy, eds., *The Jerome Biblical Commentary*. Englewood Cliffs: Prentice-Hall, Inc., 1968.

James M. Efird, *These Things Are Written*. Atlanta: John Knox Press, 1978.

Neil Fujita, *Introducing the Bible*. New York/Ramsey: Paulist Press, 1981.

F.G. Herod, *The Gospels: A First Commentary*. Atlanta: John Knox Press, 1976.

Leander Keck, *Proclamation Commentaries: Paul and His Letters*. Philadelphia: Fortress Press, 1979.

Jack Dean Kingsbury, *Proclamation Commentaries: Jesus Christ in Matthew, Mark and Luke*. Philadelphia: Fortress Press, 1981.

Gerhard Krodel, *Proclamation Commentaries: Acts*. Philadelphia: Fortress Press, 1981.

John McKenzie, *Dictionary of the Bible*. Milwaukee: The Bruce Publishing Co., 1965.

Michael Pennock, *The New Testament*. Notre Dame: Ave Maria Press, 1982.

Francis Rhein, *Understanding the New Testament.* Woodbury: Barron's Educational Series, Inc., 1974.
Merrill Unger, *Unger's Bible Dictionary.* Chicago: Moody Press, 1983.
H.L. Willmington, *Willmington's Guide to the Bible.* Wheaton: Tyndale House Publishers, Inc., 1983.

4

The Resurrection

The central doctrine of Christianity is the resurrection of Jesus. The apostle Paul put it succinctly in his First Letter to the Corinthians, "If Christ has not been raised, our preaching is void of content and your faith is empty too" (1 Cor 15:14).

From the earliest days of Christianity to our own, there have been skeptics who have denied the resurrection of Jesus. Some have said that it was a spiritual not a physical resurrection. Others claimed it was a hoax. For example, Docetists in the second century denied that Jesus had a real body and so denied Jesus' resurrection. Each century has produced its doubters. A few years ago a best seller, *The Passover Plot,* by Dr. Hugh Schonfield appeared in numerous book stores. Schonfield's main idea is that Jesus prearranged before his death to have his body removed from the tomb by people other than his apostles or disciples. Thus, he concludes that Jesus' followers were victims of Jesus' deception and this explains the early Christians' genuine belief in his resurrection. There have been similar theories proposed. None of these theories have been convincing. These works are based more on creative imagination than any hard evidence or facts.

Christians accept the resurrection as it is revealed in the New Testament. Yet, there are legitimate questions proposed by people. What are the origins of the resurrection belief? How did the apostles and disciples experience the resurrection? Did Jesus have the same body after rising from the dead? What about the empty tomb? How did Jesus look after the resurrection? These questions and others have challenged theology. However, these questions are not asked in any distrusting manner, but in order to deepen the understanding of this central mystery of faith.

The study of the resurrection of Jesus is a necessity since it is the cornerstone of the Christian faith. Without the resurrection, there is no future for the individual. The resurrection of every human being is linked with the resurrection of Jesus. If Jesus did not rise from the dead, then the Christian faith is empty and useless.

After an examination of the resurrection of Jesus, the resurrection of the dead in general will be discussed. Here again, is there any evidence from the Old and New Testaments about the resurrection of the dead?

A. THE RESURRECTION OF JESUS

The Pauline Literature

The most important evidence for the resurrection is found in Paul's First Letter to the Corinthians (A.D. 57), "I handed on to you first of all what I myself received, that

Christ died for all our sins in accordance with the Scriptures and rose on the third day; that he was seen by Cephas (Peter), then by the twelve. After that he was seen by five hundred brothers at once, most of whom are still alive, although some have fallen asleep (died). Next he was seen by James, then by all the apostles. Last of all he was seen by me, as one born out of the normal course" (1 Cor 15:3–8). Other letters of Paul describe his belief in Jesus' resurrection. A few examples will illustrate the point: (1) "It was like the strength he showed in raising Christ from the dead and seating him at his right hand in heaven" (Eph. 1:20); (2) "We believe, knowing that he who raised up the Lord Jesus will raise us up along with Jesus and place us and you in his presence" (2 Cor 4:14); (3) "If the Spirit of him who raised Jesus from the dead dwells in you, then he who raised Christ from the dead will bring your mortal bodies to live also, through his Spirit dwelling in you" (Rom 8:11); (4) "We await from heaven the Son he raised from the dead—Jesus, who delivers us from the wrath to come" (1 Thes 1:10).

The references to Jesus' resurrection in Paul's letters are very important because they are the oldest New Testament writings (A.D. 50's). Paul's encounter with the risen Jesus occurs in the Letter to the Galatians (1:11–17). This encounter with Jesus suggests a visible phenomenon. Paul's account (1 Cor 15:3–8) says that the resurrected Jesus was seen by Cephas (Peter), the twelve apostles and five hundred people. This statement sharply points out an historical event. These passages and others testify that Paul firmly believed in Jesus' resurrection: the resurrection event is described in terms of change, difference, newness and transformation. Jesus' resurrection is a pledge of one's own resurrection and a condemnation of the Jewish Sadducees who did not believe in any resurrection idea; finally, Jesus' resurrection confirms all his teachings and truly makes him the promised Messiah.

The Synoptic Gospels

The Gospels are not biographies of Jesus. They serve as testimonies confessing faith in Jesus whose words and actions proved that he was the Son of God. These evangelists are unanimous and confident in their proclamation that Jesus is the Son of God. They, like others, reflect how they understood Jesus.

Approaching the question of Jesus' resurrection from the Synoptic writers (Matthew, Mark, Luke) the task is not to demonstrate that these resurrection narratives are historical documents. Rather, it is a study to examine these confessions of faith.

Three passages (8:31; 9:31; 10:34) in Mark's Gospel record Jesus' prediction of his resurrection. Two others (9:8; 14:28) make references to the resurrection itself. One reference (26:1–8) speaks of the empty tomb.

Matthew's Gospel points out Jesus' fulfillment of the Old Testament. Within this structure, there are several references to Jesus' future resurrection (12:40; 16:4; 17:9; 20:19). One reference (28:1–20) speaks of the empty tomb.

In Luke there are only two predictions of Jesus' resurrection (9:22; 18:33). There is only one reference (24:1–12) to the empty tomb. For Luke, Jesus is the Savior of all human beings. His resurrection is essential to this plan.

Peculiar to Mark is his emphasis on the transformation that took place when Jesus rose from the dead. His body was changed: "He was revealed to them completely changed in appearance" (16:12).

Peculiar to Matthew are the following points: (1) the placing of the guards at the tomb (27:62–66); (2) the apparition of Jesus to the two women with the message of the angel (28:9f); (3) Jesus' appearance to the eleven apostles in Galilee with his final command to teach and baptize (28:16–20).

Peculiar to Luke is the fact that his account of Jesus' apparitions is much more extensive and is solely concerned with the events in and around Jerusalem.

What is common to all three Synoptic writers are these points: (1) Mt 28:1–10, Mk 16:1–8, and Lk 24:1–11 mention the empty tomb being discovered by women; (2) the resurrection was announced to the women—by a messenger (Mt), a youth (Mk), men (Lk); (3) Jesus himself appeared to the women; (4) the women announced the resurrection to the disciples.

John's Gospel

What about John's Gospel? According to John, the resurrection is a sign (miracle) that Jesus laid down his life and took it up again. It was for John the greatest sign (miracle) that Jesus performed to show that he is the Son of God. Peculiar to John are these points: (1) Peter and the beloved disciple at the empty tomb (20:2–10); (2) Jesus comes to the disciples through locked doors on the evening of the day of the resurrection (20:10–23); (3) an apparition of Jesus a week later again coming through locked doors for the benefit of Thomas (20:24–29); (4) an account of a later apparition of the risen Jesus at the Sea of Tiberias to Peter, Thomas, Nathanael, the two sons of Zebedee, and two other disciples, in connection with which there is a miraculous catch of fish, a meal on the shore and Peter's threefold statement of his love of Jesus.

The Acts of the Apostles

In Acts there are several references to the resurrection of Jesus. The main purpose of these accounts is to verify on the part of the apostles that they were witnesses to Jesus' appearances after his resurrection. Three passages (4:2; 17:31; 25:19) speak of the resurrection. Two passages (10:40; 13:30) mention that Jesus appeared to others so that they might be witnesses of his resurrection. Peculiar to Acts is a general reference to many apparitions of the risen Jesus to his disciples during the forty days after his resurrection together with the only full account of the ascension of Jesus.

In summary, all New Testament accounts have these common points about Jesus' appearances: (1) before Jesus' appearance there is fear or apprehension; (2) Jesus gives some form of greeting of peace; (3) Jesus appeared to many people; (4) all who saw Jesus were convinced that it was he; (5) Jesus commands them to go and make disciples.

A Chronological Outline

There is no definite chronological sequence of events of Jesus' resurrection in any one of the New Testament writings. For clarity, the following reconstruction is offered: (1) Jesus' appearance to Mary Magdalene at dawn on the day of the resurrection (Mk 16:9–11; Jn 20:11–18); (2) Jesus' appearance to the holy women on the day of the resurrection (Mt 28:9f); (3) Jesus' appearance on the day of the resurrection to Peter (Lk 24:34; 1 Cor 15:5); (4) Jesus' appearance on the day of the resurrection (late afternoon) to two disciples at Emmaus (Mk 16:12f; Lk 24:13–35); (5) Jesus' appearance on the day of the resurrection (late evening) to the apostles, Thomas being absent (Mk 16:14; Lk 24:36–43; Jn 30:19–23); (6) Jesus' appearance eight days later to the eleven apostles including Thomas (Jn 20:26–29); (7) Jesus' appearance to seven disciples at the Sea of Tiberias (Jn 21:1–14); (8) Jesus' appearance to the eleven apostles on a mountain in Galilee (Mt 28:16–20; Mk 16:15–18); (9) Jesus' appearance to five hundred people (1 Cor 15:6); (10) Jesus' appearance to the apostle James (1 Cor 15:7); (11) Jesus' last appearance in Jerusalem (Lk 24:44–49; Acts 1:4–8); (12) Jesus' ascension into heaven (Mk 16:19f; Lk 24:50–53; Acts 1:9–12).

The Empty Tomb Problem

Up to this point, there has been a discussion of the New Testament accounts about the appearance of Jesus after his resurrection. Now we focus on another aspect of Jesus' resurrection, namely the empty tomb.

The Gospel accounts (Mk 16:1–8; Mt 28:1–10; Lk 24:1–12; Jn 20:1–18) contain many discrepancies. Some have used the empty tomb as evidence of Jesus' resurrection. The plain fact is that an empty tomb simply tells us that the tomb was empty. The New Testament accounts testify to that fact. The Scripture writers incorporated some stories that were circulating at the time about how the tomb became empty. Some versions said that the disciples had stolen the body (Mt 28:11–15; 27:64); others said that the gardener had taken it away (Jn 20:13–15). Again, the empty tomb is not the crucial piece of evidence for Jesus' resurrection. It is simply another piece of evidence. It does verify that the tomb was empty and gives a basis for seeing a continuity between the pre- and post-resurrection body of Jesus. However, it is the appearances of Jesus after his resurrection that are most important for those who believe in his resurrection. The apostles and others had a real experience of Jesus being alive. He spoke with them and he ate with them. They touched him and had their faith enlivened by that contact. To them the resurrection of Jesus was the most overwhelming of experiences. It changed their lives and the life of our species. The resurrection of Jesus was unanimously held by all Church Fathers. The official Church condemned periodically certain people who denied the resurrection. In many cases, their denial was implicit since they denied the divinity of Christ. Among those condemned were the Cerinthians (first century), the Adoptionists (second century), Paulicians (seventh century), Albigensians (thirteenth century), the rationalists (eighteenth century), and Atheists.

The official statements on the resurrection of Jesus on the third day as being a matter of belief for all Christians is contained in the following: the Apostles' Creed, the First Council of Nicea Creed (325), the First Council of Constantinople (381), the Council of Toledo Creed (400), the Athanasian Creed (400's), the Creed of Epiphanius (400's), the Formula the "Faith of Damasus" (500's), the Formula the "Merciful Trinity" (500's), the Lateran Council Creed (649), the Fourth Lateran Council (1212), the

Second Council of Lyons Creed (1274), the Letter of Pius IV (1565), and the Letter of Pius X against Modernists (1905).

On the resurrection of Jesus' body specifically, the letter of Pope Leo IX (1053) to the bishop of Antioch, the letter of Pope Innocent III (1208) to the archbishop of Terraco, the Fourth Lateran Council (1215) and the Council of Florence (1438–1445) confirm this idea which the evangelists made clear in their accounts.

On the point that Jesus rose from the dead on his own power, the Eleventh Council of Toledo (A.D. 675) made it clear. No truth of the Christian faith is taught so clearly by the Church writers and Councils of the Church as is the resurrection. The resurrection of Jesus remains truly the keystone of the Christian faith. Without it, as Paul wrote to the Corinthians, there is no faith.

B. THE RESURRECTION OF THE DEAD

Having discussed Jesus' resurrection, our attention is focused on whether or not there will be a resurrection of the dead. We will examine Old and New Testament writings and Church documents issued through the centuries.

Old Testament Documents

In the Old Testament, the Jews believed in some form of an afterlife. They never spoke of the resurrection of the body, but only of the general resurrection of the dead due to the fact that they regarded the human being as a whole.

The earliest form of resurrection can be found in the notion of the resurrection of the nation. In the writings of the prophets, the resurrection involves a national resurrection, that is, the expectation of the restoration of Israel as a nation. The prophet Hosea (6:1f) says that if the Israelites return to Yahweh, he will revive them after two days and on the third day will raise them up to live in his presence. The prophet Ezekiel (37:1–14) portrays Israel's national restoration as a resurrection from the tomb of the exile.

Little evidence exists concerning individual resurrection which is generally found in the later writings of the Old Testament, specifically the Book of Daniel (12:2f), "Many of those who sleep in the dust of the earth shall awaken. . . ." Again, in the Second Book of Maccabees (7:9; 11:23; 14:46), the martyrdom of Jewish men, women and children under the edicts of Antiochus IV demanded God's reward for these people who remained loyal to him. Although the author of the Book of Wisdom does not explicitly mention the general resurrection of the dead, he implies it. Basically, that is the picture in the Old Testament writings about the resurrection of the dead. It becomes clearer with the teachings of Jesus. And so, again, God's revelation is gradually seen.

New Testament Documents

In the New Testament several references to the resurrection of the dead appear. Jesus resurrects the daughter of Jairus (Mt 9:18–26; Mk 5:21–42; Lk 8:40–56), the son of the widow of Naim (Lk 7:11–17); and Lazarus (Jn 11:1–44).

In the Synoptics there are two passages. Matthew's

Gospel (22:23–31) speaks of Jesus criticizing the Sadducees' belief that there is no resurrection. The Sadducees were the priests and the wealthy families of Jewish society. However, the Pharisees, the larger group of Jewish people, did believe in the resurrection. The other passage is in the Gospel of Luke (14:14). The resurrection of the just is mentioned.

The writings of Paul reflect this important teaching about the resurrection of the dead. For example, these references mention the resurrection of the dead: Rom 1:14; 4:17; 6:5; 8:11; 1 Cor 6:14; 15; 2 Cor 1:9; 4:14; 13:4; Eph 2:5; Phil 3:10; Col 2:12f; 3:1; 1 Thes 4:13–18; 1 Tim 6:13; 2 Tim 2:11–18; Heb 6:2; 11:35. Paul makes it clear that it is through the resurrection of Jesus that there is the resurrection of the dead.

The Acts of the Apostles contains Paul's sermons on the resurrection of the dead which were basically put into his letters. They can be found in these passages: 17:18–32; 23:6; 24:15–21; 26:21; 28:30.

The Gospel of John (6:39f, 44–54; 11:24) mentions the resurrection on the last day and that whoever believes in Jesus will never die. All the just will hear the voice of God and will be rewarded while the unjust will be condemned. However, John mentions in 11:25ff that Jesus corrects Martha who thinks only of the last day as the time for the resurrection of the dead.

Finally, the Book of Revelation speaks of a double resurrection. First, there will be a resurrection for the martyrs who will rule with Christ for one thousand years (20:4–6). Second, there will be a general resurrection (20:11–15).

In summary, the Jewish belief in the individual resurrection is sparse. The New Testament contains more references for the belief in the resurrection of the dead.

Questions such as "How will it take place?" "When will it
take place?" and "What type of body will I have?" are not
answered in the New Testament writings.

Church Documents

   In many ways over the centuries, the Church in official pronouncements in councils and papal encyclicals
(letters) safeguarded the truth about the resurrection of
the dead, which has its roots in the Old and New Testament writings. The Apostles' Creed says: ". . . in the resurrection of the flesh." The Creed of Epiphanius (374)
asserts: "We condemn also those who do not confess the
resurrection of the dead." The Nicean-Constantinople
Creed (381) states: "We look for the resurrection of the
dead, and the life of eternity to come." The Council of
Toledo Creed (400) says: "If anyone says and/or believes that the human bodies will not rise again after
death, let him be condemned." The Athanasian Creed
(400's) avers: "On his coming all men with their bodies
must arise." The Creed of the Eleventh Council of Toledo
(675) states: "After the example of our Head, there will be
a true resurrection of the body of all the dead." The
Fourth Lateran Council (1215) asserts: "They will arise
with their bodies which they have now." The letter of
Pope Benedict XII (1336) says, "On the day of judgment
all men with their bodies will make themselves ready to
render an account of their own deeds before the tribunal
of Christ." Finally, the Second Vatican Council (1962–
1965) in the Constitution on the Church in the Modern
World asserts: "We do not know the time for the consummation of the earth and of humanity . . . but we are

taught that God is preparing a new dwelling place and a new earth where justice will abide."

No doubt, the early Church clearly understood a resurrection of the dead, although it did not provide any detailed explanation. Such words as flesh, body and dead are employed to present the central idea of resurrection of the dead. However, while the language may not be uniform, the idea is.

A general conclusion can be made, namely, there will be a resurrection of the body, the same body that we have. The New Testament accounts mainly indicate this idea. Various conciliar and papal statements through the centuries support what Christians have always believed.

C. CONTEMPORARY THEOLOGICAL INSIGHTS

During this century, Catholic, Protestant and Orthodox Christian theologians have explored the resurrection event with new biblical knowledge. Each theologian has contributed new insights into this great Christian mystery. The work continues on. Physical, historical, and linguistic methods have helped to produce these new insights. Since the ecumenical spirit has penetrated the Christian community, these theologians have been able to exchange their views in a more open and unbiased arena. Fortunately, we are the recipients of this process. Briefly, then, we will state some of their key positions on the resurrection of Jesus.

Rudolf Bultmann believes that the resurrection of Jesus cannot be separated from his crucifixion. Together, they constitute the salvation-event of Jesus. They must not be examined separately. Besides this, for Bultmann,

all speculation about the manner of appearances of Jesus
and the discussion about the empty tomb is unimportant
and insignificant.

Raymond Brown says, first, that the categories of
space and time are human, not eschatological terms. Second, the New Testament writers tell us about the resurrection event, but they do not describe it. Third, we can
speak of a bodily resurrection of Jesus provided we understand that it was now a *different* type of body (no
longer flesh and blood).

Joseph Fitzmyer comments: (1) not to admit the resurrection of Jesus means that one is not a Christian; (2)
the New Testament writers never present the resurrection of Jesus as a resuscitation (a return to his former
body); (3) the New Testament accounts not only speak of
Jesus being alive, but also of his living influence on the
lives of his followers; (4) the bodily resurrection of Jesus
is the central theme of the New Testament preaching and
teaching.

Reginald Fuller gives the insight that the resurrection
of Jesus takes him out of the past of history and inserts
him into the eternal time period. Therefore, salvation for
any human being is not linked to the past memory of the
resurrection of Jesus, but continues here and now because of the resurrection event.

Willi Marxsen claims that the present-day Christian
can go back historically to Jesus' resurrection only to the
point that the witnesses claimed they saw the risen Jesus.
Jesus' resurrection is not an historical event, but a faith
event. Christians, therefore, are too concerned with the
details about what Jesus' resurrected body looked like,
whom he spoke to, interest in the empty tomb, and so
forth.

Dermot Lane points out that Jesus' resurrection cannot be fully understood in a biblical background, that is, biblical language (Hebrew, Aramaic, Greek) and the three levels of development behind the written Gospels.

Michael Schmaus states that the resurrection of Jesus is a reminder of God the Father's seal of love on his Son, a part of the eternal plan of salvation for humanity and a connection with one's own resurrection.

Richard McBrien says that the message of the New Testament is always the message of the resurrection. Because of the resurrection, the early Christians came to understand the divinity of Jesus.

D. GENERAL OBSERVATIONS

The resurrection of Jesus represents faith within the primitive Church. The New Testament writers have written of the experiences among the Christian community. Even Paul says explicitly that he transmits what he himself had received (1 Cor 15:3). By the time the resurrection experience is put down on paper, we see literary styles and the first formal structures emerge, such as "Christ died and was buried and rose from the dead," "he appeared to Peter and then to the twelve," and so forth. Second, the writings express the resurrection of Jesus as an elevation, a glorification, and a return to the Father. This idea conforms to the notion of the Messiah idea. Third, the resurrection of the dead will take place at the end of time. Fourth, these accounts emphasized the glorified Jesus as compared to the crucified Jesus. Fifth, the empty tomb seems to be very important for the primitive Christians. Sixth, those who saw Jesus after his resurrection experienced a living person, not a ghost or a spiritual presence. Finally, as a result of these contacts with the risen Christ, a remarkable change took place in the apostles. They were changed. No longer fearful, they were given a mission to go out and make disciples for Jesus.

What theological implications can we draw from the resurrection of Jesus? Several can be proposed: (1) the resurrection marks an approval from God about the mission of his Son Jesus; (2) the words and actions of Jesus take on a fuller meaning; (3) the divinity of Jesus is impressed on the minds of the apostles; (4) the plan of salvation for humanity is completed with Jesus' resurrection which assured our own resurrection; (5) Jesus' resurrection fulfills the Jewish apocalyptic hope of a resurrection; (6) the resurrection of Jesus means a permanent presence of Jesus in the lives of all his followers, past and present.

Therefore, the resurrection means for Catholics and many other Christians the survival of the whole human being, that is, the body and soul. It verifies once and for all the hopes and dreams of every human being to survive. Any study of the peoples of the world will show how people have hoped and planned for another life. Certainly God, in his loving plan for humanity, puts his stamp of approval on survival by the resurrection of his Son Jesus.

Summary

1. The central doctrine of Christianity is Jesus' resurrection.

2. Skeptical accounts of the resurrection of Jesus are based more on creative imagination than facts.

3. Paul's First Letter to the Corinthians is the most important evidence for the resurrection account of Jesus.

4. Paul's letters are the oldest New Testament writings.

5. The Gospels are not biographies, but testimonies about faith in Jesus.

6. There are details peculiar to each Gospel account of Jesus' resurrection.

7. Common to all three Synoptic accounts are the empty tomb, the announcement to the women, the appearance of Jesus to the women, and the women's announcement to the disciples.

8. For John the evangelist the resurrection is the greatest sign Jesus performed.

9. The Acts of the Apostles verifies that the apostles are witnesses to Jesus' resurrection.

10. There is no chronological outline of Jesus' resurrection in any one of the New Testament writings.

11. The empty tomb simply tells us that the tomb was empty.

12. For their implicit and explicit denial of Jesus' resurrection, the Cerinthians, Adoptionists, Paulicians, Albigenians, rationalists and atheists were condemned by the official Church.

13. The evangelists testify that there was a bodily resurrection of Jesus.

14. Old Testament writings speak of a general resurrection of the dead, not a resurrection of the body.

15. The New Testament writings are more specific about individual resurrections of the dead.

16. Various conciliar and papal encyclicals reaffirm the New Testament affirmation of the resurrection of Jesus and the resurrection of the dead.

17. Many Catholic, Protestant and Orthodox Christian theologians have given new insights into the resurrection of Jesus.

18. Rudolf Bultmann believes that the resurrection of Jesus cannot be separated from his crucifixion.

19. Raymond Brown says that the categories of space and time are human, not eschatological terms.

20. Joseph Fitzmyer comments that Jesus' resurrection was a living influence on the lives of his followers.

21. Reginald Fuller says that Jesus' resurrection inserts a person today into the eternal time period.

22. Willi Marxsen asserts that Jesus' resurrection is not so much an historical event as a faith event.

23. Dermot Lane points out that Jesus' resurrection can be best understood when it is placed in its biblical background.

24. Michael Schmaus states that Jesus' resurrection is God the Father's seal of love on his Son.

25. Richard McBrien says that the early Christians came to understand the divinity of Jesus because of Jesus' resurrection.

26. As a result of the apostles' contact with the risen Jesus, they were no longer fearful. They were changed.

27. The resurrection means for many Christians the survival of the whole human being.

Questions for Discussion

1. Why is the resurrection of Jesus the central doctrine of Christianity?

2. What is Schonfield's key idea?

3. Which letter of Paul is the most important for the discussion of Jesus' resurrection?

4. State three other letters of Paul which speak of Jesus' resurrection.

5. Look up one reference from the Gospels of Mark, Matthew and Luke about the resurrection of Jesus. Compare the statements.

6. Mention one point that is peculiar to Matthew about Jesus' resurrection.

7. What are the common elements in the Synoptics about Jesus' resurrection?

8. Why would there be differences in details about Jesus' resurrection event in the Synoptic Gospels?

9. Compare the accounts of Jesus' resurrection in John (20:2–29) and Luke (24:1–12).

10. What is the main idea of the Acts of the Apostles in regard to Jesus resurrection?

11. State three common points in the New Testament writings about Jesus' resurrection.

12. Discuss the accounts of Jesus on the road to Emmaus in Mark (16:12f) and Luke (24:13–35).

13. Mention the discrepancies in the Gospel accounts (Mk 16:1–8; Mt 28:1–10; Lk 24:1–12; Jn 20:1–18) concerning the empty tomb.

14. Mention three heresies against the resurrection of Jesus.

15. State three Creeds which specifically mention the resurrection of Jesus.

16. Did the Jews believe in the resurrection of the dead?

17. Mention three incidents in the New Testament writings which illustrate the resurrection of the dead.

18. Which Gospel speaks of the resurrection on the last day?

19. Compare the two types of resurrection which the Book of Revelation (20:4–15) mentions.

20. What general conclusion can be made about the resurrection of the dead?

21. What is the role of theologians in their discussions of Jesus' resurrection?

22. Discuss Fitzmyer's insights into the resurrection of Jesus.

23. Briefly list each theologian and his insight.

24. Give four general observations that can be made about the resurrection event.

25. State and discuss three theological implications about Jesus' resurrection.

Suggested Readings

Hugh Anderson, *Jesus and Christian Origins*. New York: Oxford University Press, 1964.
Raymond Brown, *The Virginal Conception and Bodily Resurrection of Jesus*. New York: Paulist Press, 1973.

Rudolf Bultmann, *Theology of the New Testament.* New York: Charles Scribner's Sons, 1951.

Joseph A. Fitzmyer, *A Christological Catechism—New Testament Answers.* New York/Ramsey: Paulist Press, 1982.

Leonard Foley, *Believing in Jesus.* Cincinnati: St. Anthony Messenger Press, 1981.

Andrew Greeley, *The Bottom Line Catechism.* Chicago: The Thomas More Press, 1982.

Monika Hellwig, *Understanding Catholicism.* New York/ Ramsey: Paulist Press, 1981.

Dermot Lane, *The Reality of Jesus.* New York/Ramsey: Paulist Press, 1980.

Richard McBrien, *Catholicism.* Minneapolis: Winston Press, 1981.

John McKenzie, *Dictionary of the Bible.* Milwaukee: The Bruce Publishing Co., 1965.

Wolfart Pannenberg, *Basic Questions in Theology, Vol. 1.* Philadelphia: The Westminister Press, 1970.

Michael Schmaus, *Dogma 3: God and His Christ.* New York: Sheed and Ward, 1971.

John Steinmueller and Kathryn Sullivan, eds., *Catholic Biblical Encyclopedia.* New York: Joseph F. Wagner, Inc., 1956.

5

Jesus' Humanity and Divinity

Before and after the birth of Jesus Christ, a remarkable number of religious leaders were born. Zoroaster
(1000 B.C.), Gautama (Buddha) and Confucius (600-500
B.C.) and Mohammed (A.D. 580's) appeared in human
history. Almost all were born within a thousand years.
However, no one claimed to be both human and divine
except Jesus. He clearly made this declaration during his
lifetime. His followers basically understood the God-Man
concept. Yet, during the first centuries of Christianity's
existence, some controversy arose concerning the hu-
manity-divinity of Jesus. These erroneous ideas (heresies)
expressed themselves in various forms. They can be divided into main groups: some who denied the humanity
of Jesus, others who denied the divinity of Jesus. The second century of Christianity witnessed no less than four-
teen heresies.

In order to understand this problem, we will look at
the issue from three areas: (1) various heresies; (2) the
writings of the Church Fathers (leaders); (3) the general
councils. This approach will allow the reader to appreciate the different aspects of this serious issue. For if Jesus
is not the God-Man, then Christianity is a hoax and a de-

ception. However, a brief review of Jesus' life and teachings will serve as an informative background for the three areas we will examine.

JESUS' LIFE AND TEACHINGS

The name Jesus is the Greek form of the Hebrew name Jehoshua. It means "to save." The name Christ is the New Testament equivalent for the Old Testament name Messiah which means "the anointed one."

While three Roman writers, Suetonius, Tacitus, and Pliny the Younger, and one Jewish writer, Josephus, of the first century mention Jesus, the Gospel accounts give much more information about him. Jesus was born at Bethlehem in the reign of the Jewish King Herod the Great (Mt 2:1; Lk 1:5). He died in the reign of Emperor Augustus Tiberius around A.D. 30 (Lk 3:13). The length of his public ministry lasted a year and a half according to the Synoptic writers, almost three years according to John's account. This discrepancy is not so important. His actions are important. On several occasions Jesus preached in synagogues (Mt 4:23; Mk 1:21; Lk 4:44). Because of large crowds and the hostility of the Jewish priests and rabbis, he spoke in open areas such as the lake shores of Galilee and other places (Mt 13:54; Lk 4:22). He was kind, articulate, strong, respectful and prayerful (Mt 7:28; Mk 1:22; Lk 4:15).

Several examples will illustrate that Jesus had a human body: (1) he became hungry and thirsty (Mt 4:2; 11:19; Jn 4:7; 19:28), slept (Mt 8:24), and became tired (Jn 4:6); (2) he became disturbed at the thought of his passion and death (Mt 26:36–46; Jn 13:21); (3) he died and his body was pierced with a lance (Jn 19:34).

His divinity is clearly seen in his miracles—for example, (1) the conversion of water into wine at Cana (Jn 2:1–11); (2) the cure of the royal official's son (Jn 4:46–53); (3) the cure of the paralytic at Capernaum (Mt 9:1–8); (4) the healing of the ten lepers (Lk 17:12–19); (5) the cure of the woman with a hemorrhage (Mk 5:24–34).

In summary, the Gospel of Mark speaks of Jesus' actions. The Gospel of Matthew talks about his concern for everyone to belong to the Kingdom of God (poor, rich, sinner, disabled, etc.). The tender human qualities of Jesus are found in Luke's Gospel. Basically, John's Gospel points out the person of Jesus himself who is the light of the world, the bread of life and the eternal life. The Acts of the Apostles testifies that the disciples of Jesus experienced Jesus the God-Man. Finally, Paul's letters generally express a central idea: Jesus the Son of God became man.

Thus the New Testament writings testify to the fact that the early Christians believed that Jesus was truly man and truly God. As Christianity developed through the centuries, controversies appeared. Several major controversies were: How can we understand the person of Jesus? How could he be man and God at the same time? Did he really have a human nature and a divine nature? These controversies rocked the Christian community. Sometimes they led to heresies. A heresy is a formal denial of any revealed truth of the Christian faith. For example, one who denies that Jesus was truly human and divine at the same time is a heretic.

For our discussion, we will divide the heresies concerning the humanity and divinity of Jesus into two general categories, namely, the denial of Jesus' humanity and the denial of his divinity. These heresies took many forms. We will consider the more important ones.

THE HUMANITY HERESIES

Gnosticism

In the early centuries some Christians questioned the humanity of Jesus, but today no one seriously questions this idea. The first major heresy of the first century was the Simonian heresy. The followers of Simon Magus, a contemporary of the apostles, denied the humanity of Jesus. His heresy was one form of the great heresy called Gnosticism. Gnosticism is a general name for a multiplicity of religious sects. Each group claimed a unique special knowledge by which one might establish contact with God. All claimed that Jesus was human only in appearance—that is, he seemed to be one of us while in reality he was not. Their main ideas were: (1) God is unknown in the sense that one in the world cannot really know him; (2) God exists in an absolute and transcendent way; (3) communication between God and humans is done by angels and Jesus is the highest and most perfect angel; (4) knowledge (revelation) comes from God only to those who are capable of being saved by it; (5) the world is evil. Other proponents of this heresy were Marcion and Valentinus of the second century.

Docetism

This heresy developed in the second and third centuries of Christianity. The main theme was that Jesus did not have a real body. He appeared to have a material body and so his sufferings and death were not real. The origins of Docetism are obscure. But it may have had its beginnings from Gnosticism. According to Basilides, a follower of this heresy, Simon of Cyrene was miraculously substituted for Jesus and crucified in his place while Jesus returned to heaven. According to Valentinian, another follower, Mary did not give birth to a real body of Jesus.

Docetism and Gnosticism heresies dominated the Christian scene during the first three centuries. However, there were others. The Manicheans were followers of Mani, a Persian from Babylonia. The Manicheans believed in many gods, rejected the Old Testament writings, and denied a real body of Jesus and free will. Another group called the Sabellians also denied the real body of Jesus.

The Early Church Fathers

In the early Christian communities, the term "Father" was generally given to Christian leaders, often clerics, who defended the Christian faith against heresies. However, many Church Fathers were laymen who were renowned for their holiness and intelligence. Their literature can be grouped into three periods. The Apostolic Era refers to the Church Fathers who had personal contact with the apostles or were instructed by their disciples—men like Clement of Rome and Ignatius of Antioch. The latter was one of the first defenders of the full humanity of Jesus. The Greek and Latin Era produced Justin, Tatian, Athenagoras and Irenaeus (Greek Fathers) and Hippolytus, Novatian and Tertullian (Latin Fathers). The reason they were called Greek and Latin Fathers was because of the language in which they wrote. Greek was the original language of the Western Church. Not until the early part of the third century did Latin become the language of the Church. Finally, the Golden Era produced many men from the four famous theological schools at Alexandria, Antioch, Edessa and Nisibis. This era occurred during the third, fourth and fifth centuries of Christianity. In the East there were Athanasius, Cyril, Basil, Gregory of Nazianus, Gregory of Nyssa, Eusebius of Caesarea, John Chrysostom and Theodore of Mopsuestia. In the West the dominant figures were Hilary of Poitiers, Ambrose of Milan, and Augustine. After this period, the number of Church Fathers declined. In part the cause lay in the great councils where the central problems of the faith were settled. In part the explanation is the political upheaval of the Christian Empire—the invasions of the barbarians in the West, and the Moslem invasion in the East. However, throughout the following centuries other Church Fathers wrote their literature. Men like John Scotus, Peter Abelard, Bonaventure and Thomas Aquinas challenged philosophical and theological heresies.

The predominant early Church Fathers against Gnosticism and Docetism were Irenaeus, Tertullian and Origen. Irenaeus was born in eastern Europe in the middle of the second century and died around 202 as the bishop of Lyons. His writing *The Detection and Overthrow of the Pretended But False Gnosis* says that Jesus took on our flesh and blood and lived as one of us. His is the God-Man who tells us about God the Father. By taking on the flesh, he became one like us. Tertullian was born in Africa around 155. He became a lawyer and was converted to Christianity in 193. It is generally believed that he became a priest. He vigorously defended the humanity of Jesus in his book *On the Flesh of Christ*. Besides this writing, he wrote many other pieces on various topics such as the soul, prayer, modesty, repentance and fasting. For Tertullian a heresy is a conscious acceptance of a doctrine which effects separation from the Christian Church. Therefore, a heresy is a decision to break with the Church over some point in its teaching. That is why he calls heretics "self-condemned." Origen was born in 185 in Eastern Europe and died in 254 as a priest at Alexandria. His work *On Principles* says, "Though born of a virgin, he truly remained God. Just as truly did he live a human life, and suffer an actual death. He also rose from the dead, spoke to those who were followers and returned bodily to the Father. The Son of God is both the Word through which the world was made, and Savior, who became human and won for men a victory over death." These Church Fathers and others like them became the first defenders of the Christian faith within the first three centuries of Christianity. Their concern was to preserve the teachings found in the New Testament.

The Divinity Heresies

By far there were many more heresies against the divinity of Jesus than his humanity. At least seven heresies occurred within the first five centuries of Christianity. One main heresy appeared in the eighth century, one in the sixteenth century, and two in the nineteenth century.

The Cerinthians of the first century were followers of Cerinthus, a contemporary of St. John. According to history, Cerinthus was an Egyptian. In Asia he founded a school where many followers accepted his ideas. They denied that God was the Creator of the world; asserted that the law of Moses was necessary for salvation; and denied the divinity of Jesus.

The Ebionites rejected all of the New Testament ex-

cept the Gospel of Matthew and denied the divinity of Jesus. They were primarily Jewish Christians who believed
that Jesus was not the Son of God but the last and greatest
of the prophets. In addition, they considered the apostle
Paul to be a heretic. The Ebionites, Alogi and Adoptionists
belonged to the second century.

The Alogi denied the authorship of the fourth Gospel
and the Book of Revelation. By denying Jesus was the
Word as John called him, they denied Jesus' divinity. Although a small group, they survived for two centuries.

The Adoptionists were followers of Theodotian, a
leather-seller of Byzantium who came to Rome. They received this title because of their solution to the Monarchianism heresy. Monarchianism stated that it could not
reconcile the divinity of Jesus with God the Father. The
Adoptionists, members of the Monarchian heresy, offered a possible solution to this problem, holding that
God adopted Jesus as his Son and raised him to the godhead. Justin, the Church Father, insisted that Jesus was
the God-Man. Jesus was not merely man, but God as well.
Jesus was truly the Son of God.

The Apollinarian, Arian and Macedonian heresies in-
fected the fourth century of Christianity. The Apollinar-
ists were started by the bishop of Laodicea. Indirectly,
they denied something of Jesus' divinity. Apollinaris
taught that Jesus had a human body and a human soul,
but no human mind. In other words, Jesus had one nature, not two natures. Some part of Jesus' divinity was
being sacrificed by Apollinaris. Athanasius and Cyril of
Jerusalem argued with Apollinaris that Jesus assumed a
complete human nature and at the same time remained
completely divine. The Arians were followers of the Alexandrian priest Arius. The basic teaching of Arianism
was the denial of the divinity of Jesus and subsequently of

the Holy Spirit. Arius reduced the Trinity to a descending triad of whom the Father alone is God. For him, Jesus was a perfect human being and *may* have been divine. This major heresy swept through the Christian communities, especially in the Eastern area of the world. Of special note is that it has its representation in the teachings of the Jehovah's Witnesses of our times. The last great heresy of the fourth century was the Macedonian. While it did not specifically deny the divinity of Jesus, it denied the divinity of the Holy Spirit. Therefore, it affected the total divinity of God (the three persons in one God). It denied the co-equality and co-eternity of the three persons in one God. And so the divinity of Jesus was affected by this idea.

In the fifth century, Nestorianism was the major heresy. Nestorius was a bishop of Constantinople. Again, it was an attack on the divinity of Jesus. His main claim was that Jesus was divine, but that Mary cannot be called the Mother of God. Rather Mary was only a woman, and God (Jesus) could not be born of a woman. Mary was the mother of the human Jesus only, but not of the divine Jesus. This heresy spread throughout the Eastern part of the world. Although many Nestorian heretics returned to orthodox teaching of the Catholic Church, some members have not. They are found today in Iraq, Iran, Syria and the United States.

The eighth century saw the reoccurrence of Adoptionism—however this time with a slight difference from the Adoptionists of the second century. This group held a double sonship in Jesus—one by generation and nature, and the other by adoption. Jesus as God is indeed the Son of God by generation and nature. Hence, the human Jesus is adopted, not the natural son of God. This form of Adoptionism originated in Spain.

The sixteenth century witnessed the Unitarian heresy. Martin Cellarius is generally regarded as the first writer of the Unitarian movement. They denied the divinity of Jesus. Modern Unitarians can trace their foundation to the sixteenth century. They grew in stages: originally in the sixteenth century, further development in England during the eighteenth century; finally in America in the nineteenth century. Today they have merged with the Universalist Church of America. Their doctrine is that they believe solely in the humanity of Jesus as a person.

The Hicksites and Christian Scientists of the nineteenth century denied the divinity of Jesus, the Trinity, the future resurrection of Christians and basic tenets of the Christian faith.

These heresies and others rocked the Christian Catholic Church from its very beginning. Twenty-one major heresies occurred before the Christian Church became official (legal). Despite this tremendous onslaught on the Christian faith, it grew and prospered through the centuries. Today, it comprises one-quarter of the world's four and one-half billion people.

In summary, the early Church Fathers' response to the heresies was: (1) the New Testament writings were reliable historical accounts; (2) the Old Testament laws were important; (3) the sacraments of the Church must be observed; (4) the basic teachings of the faith must be upheld, namely, three persons in one God (Trinity); Jesus is the Son of God, true man, true God; Mary is the Mother of God (Jesus); Jesus has two natures, two wills (human and divine); (5) salvation for the good and punishment for the wicked.

The significance of the early Church Fathers of the first five centuries was that they led the Church into full contact with the non-Christian world and made clear the

identity of the true Christian teachings. They had to investigate such questions as: Who is Jesus? How is he related to God the Father? Is the Holy Spirit God? How can
we understand the Trinity?

The early Church Fathers eventually prepared the
Church for what are called the general councils of the
Church. They are gatherings of the bishops of the Church
called together by the Pope (in the ancient Church and in
the East, the emperor summoned a council) in order to
discuss questions of faith or morals or Church discipline
or guidance. A general council or ecumenical council
consists of all the bishops of the Church from all over the
world, who have been summoned by the Pope. Their decrees became law when the Pope announces them.

The Roman Catholic Church has been in existence almost two thousand years. It was founded by Jesus Christ,
and it was Jesus who appointed Peter as its first leader
(Pope). As the Church grew in the world, it encountered
problems and it had to face them. From Peter to the present Pope John Paul II, each Pope has had the responsibility of Jesus' command: "All power is given to me in
heaven and on earth. Go, therefore, teach all nations,
baptizing them in the name of the Father, and the Son,
and the Holy Ghost, teaching them to observe all things
whatsoever I have commanded you; and behold I am
with you all days even to the consummation of the world"
(Mt 28:18–20).

Because of human problems and doctrinal controversies, the authorities of the Church have had to settle
these matters. In its long history, the Church has had
twenty-one general or ecumenical councils. However, it
was not until the fourth century (325) that the Church had
its first general council.

Until the fourth century, "councils" were really

groups of bishops of small areas who met to discuss pastoral practice, or to decide on the authenticity of the books of the Bible. A "general" or "ecumenical" Council is supposed to have representatives from all Christian communities. This has always been an ideal not actually accomplished because doctrinal or political disputes often prevented some groups from being represented at the councils. There are twenty-one councils recognized by the Roman Catholic Church. This means that the teachings of these councils are binding on Catholics unless the Pope vetoes the teaching. Almost all Christians recognized the teachings of the ancient councils as binding.

The twenty-one general councils made the following official statements about the basic teachings of Christianity.

Fourth Century: First Ecumenical Council: **Nicea** (325) condemned the heresy of Arius, an Alexandrian priest, who denied the divinity of Jesus.

Second Ecumenical Council: **Constantinople** (381) condemned Macedonius who denied the divinity of the Holy Spirit, and Apollinaris, a bishop, who claimed that Jesus had a human body, but no human mind.

Fifth Century: Third Ecumenical Council: **Ephesus** (431) stated that Mary was the Mother of the human and divine person of Jesus. Nestorius and his followers, who denied that Mary should be called "Mother of God" were condemned.

Fourth Ecumenical Council: **Chalcedon** (451) emphasized that Jesus had a human and a divine nature.

Sixth Century: Fifth Ecumenical Council: **Constantinople II** (553) denied the idea that human beings were pure spirits. It also condemned the "Three Chapters" of the Nestorians.

Seventh Century: The Sixth Ecumenical Council: **Constantinople III** (680–681) condemned Monothelitism, the doctrine that Christ had only one will. Monothelitism was an attempt to unite the factions in the Eastern Church, especially the Monophysites who taught Christ had only one nature.

Eighth Century: The Seventh Ecumenical Council: **Nicea II** (787) taught that Christians could venerate the images of the saints. The Moslems had conquered much of the East and condemned all forms of idolatry; there was much political pressure to conform to their practice.

Ninth Century: The Eighth Ecumenical Council: **Constantinople IV** (869–879), under pressure from the Pope, condemned the Patriarch Photius' irregular elevation to the see of Constantinople. This action eventually caused the Greek schism.

Twelfth Century: The Ninth Ecumenical Council: **Lateran I** (1123) confirmed the Concordat of Worms, which settled disputes between the Pope and the Western Emperor on questions about authority and control, and about the election of bishops.

The Tenth Ecumenical Council: **Lateran II** (1139) ended the Western schism caused by the false Pope Anacletus II. It condemned certain ideas, such as that there are only two sacraments (baptism and the Eucharist), and also the rejection of the baptism of infants.

The Eleventh Ecumenical Council: **Lateran III** (1179) confirmed the papal treaty with the emperor. It ruled that a majority of two thirds of the cardinals' votes were needed to elect a Pope. It rejected the idea that only the New Testament and not the Old was inspired, and that there are two Gods.

Thirteenth Century: The Twelfth Ecumenical Council: **Lateran IV** (1215) condemned the sect of the Cathari.

It defined the doctrine of transubstantiation, that is, that consecrated bread and wine changes into the body and blood of Christ even though the appearances remain the same. This council obliged Catholics to go to confession and Communion at least once a year.

The Thirteenth Ecumenical Council: **Lyons I** (1245) confirmed the Pope's deposition of the Western emperor and it organized a general crusade.

The Fourteenth Ecumenical Council: **Lyons II** (1274) created a short-lived reunion with the Greek Church. It set up a new crusade, and approved the new regulations for electing a Pope.

Fourteenth Century: The Fifteenth Ecumenical Council: **Vienna** (1311–1312) confirmed the abolition of the military order, the Knights Templar. It intervened in the quarrel between branches of the Franciscans about the vow of poverty.

Fifteenth Century: The Sixteenth Ecumenical Council: **Constance** (1414–1418) ended the Great Western Schism and elected Martin V the true Pope. It condemned the reformed teachings of John Wycliffe and of John Hus, who taught that the Church is made up of people who are predestined. Hus was put to death as a heretic in 1415. It stated that a general council was superior to a Pope and wanted councils held regularly. The Pope refused to accept this doctrine of "conciliarism."

The Seventeenth Ecumenical Council: **Basel-Ferrara-Florence** (1431-1445) featured the struggle of Pope Eugene to overcome conciliarism. He secured another temporary union with the Greek Church.

Sixteenth Century: The Eighteenth Ecumenical Council: **Lateran V** (1512–1517) condemned the schismatic Council of Pisa. It settled questions about the human soul and made some small attempts at reform, but really did not correct major abuses.

The Nineteenth Ecumenical Council: **Trent** (1545–1563) made genuine reform. It condemned the erroneous teachings of Luther, Calvin, Zwingli and other reformers, but left open the possibility of dialogue with the reformers in the future on open issues. It restructured the Church and gave official teachings about the Bible and tradition, original sin and justification, the seven sacraments, the Sacrifice of the Mass, and the cult of saints. In many ways it "froze" theology and liturgy.

Nineteenth Century: The Twentieth Ecumenical Council: **Vatican I** (1869–1870) defined the primacy of the Pope and the infallibility of the Pope in matters of faith and doctrine.

Twentieth Century: The Twenty-First Ecumenical Council: **Vatican II** (1962–1965) was a pastoral council which re-examined Church discipline, restored the vernacular language to the liturgy, revised the sacramental rites, stressed the importance of the laity, and opened dialogue with non-Catholics.

These general councils received their name from the place in which they met. They state what the official Church holds.

Having looked briefly at the twenty-one general councils and their statements about the Christian faith, we will examine more closely the general statements of three major councils about the person of Jesus.

The *Council of Nicea* (325), composed of three hundred bishops, condemned the denial of the divinity of Jesus made by Arius, an Alexandrian priest. This heresy began in Africa and Egypt. Arius held that Jesus was merely a human being. Athanasius, a bishop of Alexandria, led the battle against this idea. After much discussion, the council adopted the following Creed: "We believe in one God, the Father, the Almighty, maker of heaven and earth, of all that is, seen and unseen. We believe in one Lord, Jesus Christ, the only Son of God, eternally begotten of the Father, God from God, Light from Light, true God from true God, begotten, not made, one in Being with the Father. Through him all things were made. For us men and for our salvation he came down from heaven; by the power of the Holy Spirit he was born of the Virgin Mary and became man. For our sake he was crucified under Pontius Pilate; he suffered, died, and was buried. On the third day he rose again in fulfillment of the Scriptures; he ascended into heaven and is seated at the right hand of the Father. He will come again in glory to judge the living and the dead, and his kingdom will have no end. We believe in the Holy Spirit, the Lord, the giver of life, who proceeds from the Father and the Son; with the Father and the Son he is worshiped and glorified. He has spoken through the prophets. We believe in one holy catholic and apostolic Church. We acknowledge one baptism for the forgiveness of sins. We look for the resurrection of the dead and the life of the world to come."

Although the Nicean Creed affirmed the divinity of the Son, it remained silent about the distinction between the Father, the Son, and the Holy Spirit. This problem was discussed and settled by the Council of Chalcedon (451). However, in between the Council of Nicea and the Council of Chalcedon, another problem had to be settled—the Nestorian heresy. Nestorius, the bishop of Constantinople, stated that Mary was the Mother of Jesus' human nature, but was not the Mother of his divine nature.

The *Council of Ephesus* (431) was called and condemned Nestorius. The fathers of this council actually made no new formula of belief. Rather, they settled a belief that was already contained in the Nicean Creed. Approximately two hundred fathers issued the following statement: "One and the same is the eternal Son of the Father and the Son of the Virgin Mary, born in time after the flesh; therefore, she may rightly be called Mother of God." To sum up, Ephesus' importance was a simple repeat of Nicea. On October 11, 1931, the Roman Catholic Church established the Feast of the Maternity of Mary.

The *Council of Chalcedon* (451) put an end to the bitter disputes which erupted between the Council of Nicea and the Council of Ephesus. It condemned the Monophysitism which taught that Jesus had one nature (not two, human and divine as the Church had taught). The final formula or creed was expressed in this way: "Therefore, following the holy Fathers, we all with one voice teach that it should be confessed that our Lord Jesus Christ is . . . truly God and truly man . . . of one substance with the Father as to his Godhead, and at the same time of one substance with us as regards his manhood . . . recognized in two natures, without confusion, without separation, not as parted into two persons, but one and the same Son." Jesus has a human nature and a divine nature. While the Creed of Chalcedon reflects the teachings of Scripture and the early tradition of the Church, it helped to spur on future theological reflection.

General Observations

In conclusion, Jesus is the founder of Christianity. We cannot understand the Jesus of history and the Jesus of faith unless we examine the past. We cannot be indifferent to any age. Each age contributed insights into the person of Jesus.

Despite the heresies that arose in the first centuries, the divinity and the humanity of Jesus were preserved in the Creeds from the general councils of Nicea, Ephesus and Chalcedon. These Creeds preserve the pure picture of Christ as it was stated in the New Testament writings. They express stages of growth of the Church. The Constitution on the Church of the Second Vatican Council says: "This is the unique Church of Christ which in the Creed we avow as one, holy, catholic and apostolic. After his resurrection our Savior handed it over to Peter to be shepherded, commissioning him and the other apostles to propagate and govern it. He set it up for all ages as 'the pillar and mainstay of the truth.' This Church, constituted and organized in the world as a society, persists in the Catholic Church, which is governed by the successor of Peter and by the bishops in union with that successor, although many elements of sanctification and of truth can be found outside of its visible structure. These elements belong to the Catholic Church and possess an inner dynamism toward Catholic unity."

Summary

1. Within a thousand years, the religious leaders Zoroaster, Gautama, Mohammed, Confucius and Jesus were born.

2. Jesus, in Hebrew Jehoshua, means "to save."

3. Christ in Greek means "the anointed one."

4. The Roman writers Suetonius, Tacitus, and Pliny the Younger and the Jewish writer Josephus mention the historical Jesus.

5. Human traits of hunger, thirst, fear and sleep are attributed to Jesus to prove his humanity.

6. Jesus' divinity is shown by his numerous miracles.

7. The New Testament writings express their belief in the humanity and divinity of Jesus.

8. The Gnosticism heresy claimed that special knowledge was necessary for salvation.

9. The Simonian heresy was one of the various types of Gnosticism.

10. The Docetism heresy stated that Jesus did not have a real body.

11. The Gnosticism and Docetism heresies dominated the first three centuries of Christianity.

12. The Manichean and Sabellian heresies denied the humanity of Jesus.

13. Church Fathers (Church leaders) were either clergymen or laymen.

14. The Apostolic Era of Church Fathers meant that they were in direct or indirect contact with the apostles' teachings.

15. The Greek and Latin Era produced Justin, Athenagoras, Irenaeus, Hippolytus, Novatian and Tertullian.

16. The Golden Era witnessed four famous theological schools at Alexandria, Antioch, Edessa and Nisibis.

17. Throughout Christianity there has been Church Fathers' literature.

18. Tertullian, Irenaeus and Origen were the primary Church Fathers against Gnosticism and Docetism.

19. There were more heresies against the divinity of Jesus than against his humanity.

20. Cerinthians, Ebionites, Alogi, Adoptionists, Arians, Macedonians, Nestorians, Unitarians, Hicksites and Christian Scientists denied the divinity of Jesus either directly or indirectly.

21. The primary aim of the early Church Fathers was to defend the humanity and divinity of Jesus.

22. The main significance of the early Church Fathers was to identify the true Christian teachings.

23. General councils (ecumenical councils) are gatherings of bishops called by the Pope (by the emperor in the East during the early centuries).

24. There have been twenty-one general (ecumenical) councils in the twenty centuries of Christianity.

25. The names of general councils come from the place in which they meet.

26. The Council of Nicea (325) was the first major general council of Christianity.

27. The Council of Ephesus (431) reaffirmed the teaching of the Council of Nicea with an additional fact: Mary was the Mother of Jesus' human and divine natures.

28. The Council of Chalcedon (451) stated that Jesus had a human and divine nature.

29. The general councils of Nicea, Ephesus and Chalcedon defended the divinity and humanity of Jesus.

30. Each age of Christianity contributes insights into the person of Jesus.

Discussion Questions

1. Who were the five great religious leaders who lived within a thousand years?

2. What does the name Jesus Christ mean?

3. Name the pagan writers who mention the historical Jesus.

4. Give several examples from Scripture to prove the humanity of Jesus.

5. What is a heresy?

6. What is Gnosticism? What were their main ideas?

7. What was the Docetism heresy? What were Basilides' and Valentinian's ideas?

8. Explain the Apostolic Age, the Greek-Latin Era, and the Golden Age of the Church Fathers.

9. Why are the Church Fathers called Greek or Latin Fathers?

10. Identify two Greek and two Latin Church Fathers.

11. Identify the four theological schools during the first five centuries of Christianity.

12. Who was Irenaeus? Briefly describe his three writings.

13. Briefly identify the Cerinthians, Ebionites, Alogi, Adoptionists, Apollinarians, Arians, Macedonians, Nestorians, Unitarians, Hicksites and Christian Scientists.

14. What is the relationship between the Adoptionists and Monarchians?

15. Where do Nestorians live today?

16. State the five major points of all Church Fathers.

17. What was the main significance of the early Church Fathers' writings?

18. State the main theme of the general councils of Constantinople I, Ephesus, Chalcedon, Constantinople III, Lateran II, Trent and Vatican II.

19. Discuss any five general councils.

20. Class project: Discuss each section of the Nicean Creed.

21. What was the importance of the general councils of Ephesus and Chalcedon?

22. Discuss the statement, "He (Jesus) set it (the Catholic Church) up for all ages as the pillar and mainstay of the truth."

Suggested Readings

Hugh Anderson, *Jesus and Christian Origins*. New York: Oxford University Press, 1964.

Henry Bettenson, ed., *Documents of the Christian Church*. New York: Oxford University Press, 1970.

Henry Chadwick, *The Early Church*. London: Penguin Books, Ltd., 1973.

Henry Denzinger, *The Sources of Catholic Dogma*. St. Louis: B. Herder Book Co., 1957.

Joseph Fitzmyer, *A Christological Catechism—New Testament Answers*. New York/Ramsey: Paulist Press, 1982.

Aloys Grillmeier, *Christ in Christian Tradition*. New York: Sheed and Ward, 1965.

John Hardon, *The Catholic Catechism*. Garden City: Doubleday & Company, Inc., 1975.

John Knox, *The Humanity and Divinity of Christ*. Cambridge: Cambridge University Press, 1981.

J.B. Lightfoot, *The Apostolic Fathers*. Michigan: Baker Book House, 1965.

Richard McBrien, *Catholicism*. Minneapolis: Winston Press, 1981.

J. Neuner and H. Rood, *The Teaching of the Catholic Church*. Staten Island: Alba House, 1967.

G. O'Collins, *What Are They Saying About Jesus?* New York/Ramsey: Paulist Press, 1977.

Maxwell Staniforth, trans., *Early Christian Writings*. England: Penguin Press, 1968.

P. Verbraken, *The Beginnings of the Church*. New York/Ramsey: Paulist Press, 1968.

6

The Shroud of Turin

Introduction

In the Cathedral of St. John the Baptist at Turin, Italy, stands the black marble Royal Chapel designed by Guarino Guarini which was once the place of private worship for the dukes of Savoy, former rulers of Italy. Above the ornate black marble altar, preserved in a rectangular glass case is an ivory-colored linen Shroud. Because of age, the linen cloth is almost yellow-colored. The cloth measures about 14½ feet long and 3½ feet wide. Burn and water marks from a fire in 1532 run down the cloth's sides. On the cloth are two distinct impressions of a body. One is the front of a man's body; the other is his back, the two images lying head to head with a space of about six inches between them. The body imprint is that of a well-built man, mid-thirties, 5 feet 11 inches tall, approximately 170 pounds, Caucasian, shoulder-length hair, a mustache and a short beard. The face is owl-like; the eyes are closed; the feet appear to be missing from the frontal image; the legs, thighs, knees and calves are visible and the hands are folded over the pelvis. The images of this nude body show lesions from severe beatings on the face, cheeks, wrists and other parts of the body. Around the head of the man, small lesions appear.

Since the Shroud's appearance in the fourteenth century, controversies have arisen about its authenticity. Is it the burial cloth of Jesus Christ or a fake? Never has there been such interest since an Italian photographer, Secondo Pia, photographed the cloth for the first time in 1898. When he developed his photographic plates, he discovered that the image on them was not a negative but a positive image. In other words, what Pia was looking at were positive images and what he saw on the cloth were negative images. He believed the Shroud belonged to Jesus Christ.

Professors Paul Vignon and Yves Delage of the Sorbonne University in Paris presented to the French Academy of Science on April 21, 1902 a report with these conclusions: (1) the image on the Shroud could not have been painted; (2) the image was actually the imprint of a human body; (3) the man of the Shroud was Jesus Christ.

The findings of this report have stirred scientists, historians, pathologists and Church officials to investigate the Shroud dilemma. Almost no one is neutral. Either one accepts the Shroud as authentic, that is, the actual burial cloth of Jesus Christ, or one believes it to be a complete fake.

Historical View

To understand this controversy, we need to know a bit of the historical development of the Shroud. For the past six hundred years the documentation on the Shroud is well known. What happened prior to the fourteenth century can be loosely reconstructed.

During the first century, the Shroud was taken for safety to the city of Edessa in Eastern Europe (now Urfa in Turkey). There it was placed in the Cathedral of Holy Sophia. For six centuries, the Greeks venerated it. In fact, they called it the mandylion (a Greek word meaning cloth). Then the Moslems invaded Edessa, but the Shroud remained safe. Not until the tenth century do we hear that the Shroud was transferred from Edessa to the chapel of the Pharaohs at Constantinople in Turkey. In the thirteenth century, the crusaders sacked Constantinople, destroying church buildings and confiscating religious treasures. Mysteriously the Shroud disappeared. An historical account says that the secretive order of the Knights Templar took it to France.

From this point, the historical record of the Shroud is more reliable. In the fourteenth century the De Charny family of Lirey, France acquired the Shroud. The first known public exposition of the Shroud took place in Lirey. Interestingly, Pierre D'Arces, bishop of Troyes, declared the Shroud a forgery. For some unknown reason, Margaret de Charny gave the Shroud to the House of Savoy. In 1503 Chamery, France was designated as the Shroud's permanent home. The Shroud was placed over the high altar of the Sainte Chapelle in Chamery, and, suddenly on December 4, 1532, a fire broke out in the chapel and the Shroud was damaged. Two years later the damaged Shroud, which the Poor Claire nuns repaired, was returned to the chapel. Turin, Italy became the new home of the Shroud in 1578. But it was not until 1694 that the Shroud was placed in the Royal Chapel of Turin Cathedral. From that time until now, the Shroud has remained there. There was one exception because of the Second World War (1939–1945). The Shroud was brought to the crypt of the Benedictine Monastery of Monte Vergine in Avellino, Italy (140 miles south of Rome). In 1946 Cardinal Fassati brought the Shroud back from Avellino to Turin.

Recently, three major scientific commissions (1969, 1973, 1977) examined the Shroud for its authenticity. The results created more questions than answers. A final note to the historicity of the Shroud is that the Vatican became its owner when the former king of Italy, Umberto II, died in 1983. He willed the Shroud to the Vatican and it is no longer the property of the House of Savoy. However, the Vatican allows the Shroud to remain in Turin.

Scriptural View

If the Shroud is authentic, the imprint of the body must conform with the details of the Gospel accounts of Jesus' passion. Some biblical scholars speak of a complete ritualistic burial which included washing and anointing of the body. This would seem to eliminate the possibility of an imprint like that on the Shroud of Turin. However, other scholars say that the Scriptures signify a hasty, provisional burial without washing and anointing.

For clarity, we will examine four areas: the practice of crucifixion during Jesus' time, the instruments of crucifixion, the crucifixion of Jesus, and the burial customs of Jews and the Gospel accounts of Jesus' burial. After these considerations, our attention will be focused on the medical and scientific evaluation of the Shroud.

First, the crucifixion was intended as a severe punishment and a frightful deterrent method of capital punishment. Unlike the Greeks, the Romans frequently practiced it. The earliest historical record of crucifixion goes back to the Persian period (sixth century B.C.). From the Persians the form of execution spread to the Phoenicians, the Egyptians, the Carthaginians and the Romans. Crucifixion was finally banned by Constantine the Great, the first Christian emperor, in 337.

During the wars the Romans started to crucify deserters, thieves and rebels. According to the Jewish historian Josephus, five hundred Jews were crucified by the Romans from the death of Herod the Great (4 B.C.) to the destruction of Jerusalem (A.D. 70). While Josephus' account might be over-exaggerated, little doubt remains that many Jews were crucified by the Romans during their occupation of Palestine.

In times of peace, crucifixion was reserved primarily for slaves. The Roman writers Livy and Tacitus mention the revolt of Spartacus. Six thousand crosses marked the road from Capua to Rome. Normally Roman citizens were never crucified. It was a privilege of Roman citizenship. However, the Roman writer Cicero writes that crucifixion was done with some regularity but only to "new citizens," namely people who were either emancipated slaves or provincials.

Second, the instruments of crucifixion were basic with a few variations depending on the circumstances. Three types of crosses were used; the X form; the T form and the form on which Jesus was crucified. According to historical records, the prisoner was stripped and scourged at the place of condemnation. A crossbeam was placed on the shoulders of the condemned, who was then fastened to the cross, either with ropes or with nails through the wrists. Then he walked to the place of execution, at which time the upright beam lay on the ground. The crossbeam was then fastened to it, and the feet were either nailed or roped to the upright beam. The hands were fastened by ropes or nails to the crossbeam. The body was supported by either a wooden seat of some kind halfway up the upright beam or by a horizontal wooden piece for the feet three quarters of the way down the upright beam. Nails seem to have been the usual method. Experts say that three or four nails were sufficient for a rapid and firm crucifixion. The height of the cross varied. Death came within a few hours or several days, depending on the loss of blood from the scourging and especially the nailing. Eventually the prisoner died by asphyxiation.

Third, how was Jesus crucified? Because of respect for the Jewish sense of public decency, the Romans did not force Jesus to walk naked through the streets of Jerusalem. After his scourging, Jesus was given his clothes when he was led out to Golgotha (Mt 27:31ff). He was allowed to wear a loincloth on the cross after he was stripped of his garments at the place of execution (Golgotha). Likewise, the giving of stupefying drink to a man condemned to death was a concession to the Jews by the Romans though Jesus refused to drink (Mk 15:23ff). Inasmuch as Jesus was led to Golgotha fully clothed, his arms would not have been fastened to the crossbeam until he was stripped at the place of execution. However, according to Roman practice he was made to carry the crossbeam (Jn 19:17), though on the way Simon of Cyrene was made to carry it for Jesus because Jesus became very weak (Mt 27:32ff). The Shroud of Turin shows that the nailing was done through the wrist which would have supported the body. Historical records verify this procedure. In the case of Jesus, a title was placed above his head (Mt 27:37; Lk 23:38; Jn 19:19). Each of the Gospel writers has a slightly different version of the inscription. However, John's account (19:19) is probably the closest to the actual wording: Jesus of Nazareth, King of the Jews. As far as the crowning of thorns, in Jesus' case it was done because of the charge (Jesus was a king).

Normally, the Romans allowed the corpse to remain on the cross and to be devoured by vultures and wild dogs. However, the bodies could be asked for by the families who wished to bury their loved ones. Very rarely was this request granted. Out of respect for the religious practices of the Jews, which forbade the body to remain beyond sunset, the Romans gave permission to have Jesus' body taken down from the cross and to be buried.

Fourth, the Jews attached great importance to burials. To remain unburied was the greatest misfortune (Eccl 6:3). The importance of a burial was attached to the idea that survival after death depends on having the body preserved in some way. The prophet Daniel writes: "Many of those who have already died will live again; some will enjoy eternal life, and some will suffer eternal disgrace" (12:2). In New Testament times, the Pharisees believed in a resurrection but the Sadducees did not.

As far as funeral customs are concerned, the eyes of the deceased were closed. The body was washed and anointed with spices and wrapped in linen cloths (1 Sam 1:2–3). Likewise in New Testament times the same procedure continued (Acts 9:37; Jn 12:7; 19:39f; Mk 15:46f; Lk 23:53f). Of special note is the fact that the corpse was dressed with white garments with sleeves. The use of the Shroud became a later custom, about two centuries before Jesus' birth.

In the case of Jesus' burial, the Gospel accounts are basically the same with some minor differences. According to the Synoptic Gospels (Mt 27:59; Mk 15:46; Lk 23:53) the body of Jesus was wrapped in a shroud, whereas according to John's account (19:40f) it was wrapped in a linen cloth and a piece of small linen, like a handkerchief, was placed over his face (20:7). Many Greek philologists say that the Greek words of John do not mean two separate pieces of cloth, but one piece. Nowhere in the other accounts is there mention of strips of cloth, bandages such as bound the hands and feet of Lazarus in the tomb (Jn 11:44). Two evangelists (Jn 12:7; Lk 23:53) mention that spices were brought to the tomb to anoint Jesus' body. Matthew and Mark do not say anything about the anointing. A final point concerning the spices used for the anointing of Jesus' body: John's account (19:38–39) says, " . . . and Nicodemus also came bringing a mixture of myrrh and aloes, about a hundred pound weight." Myrrh is a red aromatic gum resin obtained from south Arabia. Myrrh dissolved in oil was one of the ingredients of the burial anointing oil. Together with aloes (an expensive scented power), Jesus' body was anointed. Luke mentions spices which can only mean myrrh and aloes. These two spices were normally used for the temporary preservation of the body in burial cases.

The burial of Jesus took place immediately because of the beginning of Passover and the Jewish law (Dt 21; 23) which insisted upon burial before sunset (Mt 27:57–66; Mk 15:42–47; Lk 23:50–56; Jn 19:32–42).

Whether the Shroud of Turin belongs to Jesus or not will be discussed later. At this point, the Scripture accounts of Jesus' crucifixion and burial are clear. The man of the Shroud displays bruises around the head, shoulders and the entire body. He was also crucified.

Medical and Scientific View

According to Roman Law, non-citizens like Jesus received a scourging with whips made of leather or chain lashes which were often fixed with sharp objects such as small pieces of bone or weighted at their ends with little lead balls. Jesus' scourging took place not inside but outside the Roman praetorium, in public. After he was scourged, he was brought into the praetorium for the crowning of thorns (Mt 27:27; Mk 15:16; Jn 19:2). These wounds would seem consistent with the small lesions around the head of the man of the Shroud. Likewise, another consistency exists. Many small wounds over the entire body front and back conform to the wounds Jesus received when he was scourged (Mt 27:26; Mk 15:15; Lk 23:16; Jn 19:1).

All four evangelists (Mt 27:33f; Mk 15:24f; Lk 23:33; Jn 19:17–18) state that Jesus was crucified. However, they do not elaborate whether it was done by nails or ropes. We have mentioned that both practices were done by the Romans. The resurrection accounts of John (20:20, 25, 27) and of Luke (24:40) indicate that Jesus' hands and feet were nailed. The wounds caused by nails would account for the bloodstains that appear on the forearms of the man of the Shroud. According to John's Gospel (19:31–37), Jesus' side was pierced by the Roman soldier's lance. The man of the Shroud has a wound with a large bloodstain around the rib cage on the right side. Finally, the Shroud shows bruise marks around the face. The evangelists (Mt 26:68; Mk 14:65; Lk 22:63–64; Jn 18:22) say that Jesus was slapped several times during his interrogation.

Three questions can be asked. What about the

bloodstains—are they real bloodstains or red painted marks? Were the body impressions caused by a scorching technique? Can the photographs be fakes?

The first question about the bloodstains has been given great consideration by doctors around the world. Dr. Bucklin of America states, "Each of the different wounds acted in characteristic fashion. Each bled in a manner which corresponded to the nature of the injury. The blood followed the flow of gravity in every instance." Dr. Willis of England claims that the injuries of the man of the Shroud are in harmony with the injuries of Jesus. The Shroud shows: (1) swelling of both eyes, (2) torn right eyelid, (3) large swelling of both eyebrows, (4) swollen nose, (5) swelling of the left cheek, and (6) swelling to the left side of the chin. All these injuries would have been sustained by Jesus during his interrogation by the Jewish high priest and Pilate's soldiers. Dr. Barbet of France notes that about a teaspoon of water (pericardial fluid) would be present in a corpse. If the corpse sustained severe beatings, then larger amounts would be present. The man of the Shroud exhibits large amounts of pericardial fluid. Dr. Barbet concludes that St. John's Gospel (19:33–36) describes vividly the blood and water flowing from Jesus' side which was pierced by the Roman soldier's lance.

These injuries would have produced bloodstains. Medical experts claim that the formation of bloodstains on the Shroud corresponds to blood formed when it clots on the skin with a concentration of the red corpuscles around the edge of the clot. Many concluded that the Shroud reveals that the bloodstains were made from human blood. Their conclusions were reached after performing bile pigment, hemochromogen, cyanomethemoglobin, albumin and protein tests. In addition, the bloodstains on the Shroud have a special color, almost vivid red. They vary in depth and intensity giving the appearance of varying thickness. Another important feature is that the bloodstains have a definite precise outline despite the merging imperceptible form left by the body.

Among those who do not share the idea that the bloodstains came from human blood is Dr. Walter McCrone, a renowned microscopist. He believes that these stains are iron oxide residue from paint used to create the body images found on the Shroud. Samuel Pellicori, an optical physicist and spectroscopist, says, "The red color (on the Shroud) is startlingly reminiscent of recent blood and not at all what one would expect after a minimum of six hundred years. . . . The color of the bloodstains on the Shroud remains a mystery." However, the consensus among medical and scientific professions is that the bloodstains on the Shroud have come from human blood, not paint. Whether the bloodstains belong to Jesus or to another is another question. They argue that it would be impossible to remove every particle of paint out of the intertwining threads of the fabric. Furthermore, the fluid part of the paint would have spread along some of the threads of the linen and not others.

Were the impressions of the man of the Shroud produced by a scorching technique? Could that account for the Shroud image which fades and blurs when viewed closer than six feet? The Shroud shows no brush marks. Some say that scorching by heat was used to produce the image on the Shroud. The problem with this solution seems to be that today's technology has not mastered this technique. Could a forger in the Middle Ages do it? Hardly.

Finally the question is asked: Are the photographs a fake? Dr. Max Frei, a noted Swiss criminologist, pub-

lished an article in 1955 on the faking of the photographs
of the Shroud. In 1973, during his examination of the photographs of the Shroud, he noticed that the surface of the
cloth was covered with minute dust particles. He received permission to remove some particles from the surface of the Shroud. He found that these particles came
from typical halophyte plants common to the desert regions around the Jordan Valley. Since 1973, he has identified forty-nine species of plants whose pollens are
represented on the Shroud. Several scientists share his
view.

Opinions

We have come to the most fascinating section of this
chapter. What do the experts say? Can they settle the
problem? The most common opinions will give an insight
into the problem.

First, in the case of normal portrait photography, the
face when reversed on the negative will appear grotesque
because the areas that were in light show up as dark
tones. When the negative is exposed, these light areas
are reversed to produce once again a lifelike picture. In
the case of the image on the Shroud, the face and body
are not lifelike on the cloth itself. They become lifelike
when their light areas are reversed by a photographic
negative. It has been suggested that the Shroud itself is a
photographic negative. The Shroud's negativity was perhaps created accidentally or deliberately by some early
artist. The question has to be asked why should some unknown forger have gone to elaborate lengths to produce
an image of being seen?

Second, the bloodstains on the Shroud seem to be real blood; they flow in the wrong direction if they occurred while Jesus lay in the tomb. Also, the bloodstains on the Shroud have not been demonstrated to belong to the first century. McCrone's position that the bloodstains were made by paint, a mixture of iron oxide and mercury sulfide, has not received acceptance from the scientific community because they have not been able to confirm McCrone's findings by experimentation.

Third, an artist of the Middle Ages could not have painted the image on the Shroud, and he would have had to crucify someone to get the pathophysiology correctly. How could he have done it since the Emperor Constantine in the fourth century outlawed crucifixion and Eastern and Western art depictions of crucifixions are medically incorrect.

Fourth, Dr. Frei's deduction about the dust particles of the Shroud coming from plants of the first century in Palestine has attracted worldwide attention. While it is possible to argue that a medieval century forger may have obtained a genuine Palestinian cloth for his purpose, this argument must be considered extremely improbable.

Fifth, the coin problem creates more complications. Sometimes coins were placed on the eyes of the deceased during these early centuries. The Jews copied this practice from the Greeks. However, we do not know if it was universally practiced by the Jews. Professor Robert Haralick of Virginia Polytechnic Institute claims that through his computer investigation of the Shroud, his photographs show the Pontius Pilate coin image. Many experts claim that the image of this coin is simply a blur. They discount his findings. Another point against the probability of placing a coin on the eyes of Jesus would be the Jewish hatred for the Romans. They certainly would not have used a Roman coin. Maybe a Jewish coin? Possible, but highly unlikely.

Sixth, the scorching theory basically is rejected by experts because modern artists have not mastered this technique. How could a medieval artist have? Besides, to scorch a piece of cloth will invariably cause burn holes in the cloth.

Seventh, a modern investigator, Joe Nickell, reproduced many aspects of the Shroud image by applying a mixture of myrrh and aloes. His conclusion is that the Shroud is a forgery. Opposition to his theory is centered on the lack of this modern technique in the medieval days.

Eighth, there is the Scripture argument based on tradition. Tradition says that Jesus was washed. In the Church of the Holy Sepulcher there is a reddish colored rectangular stone on which Jesus is said to have been laid for the washing and anointing. While many Scripture scholars hold that Jesus was washed because of the traditional Jewish burial custom, the Gospels do not specifically mention it. The argument against the washing is based on the fact that Jesus died around 3 P.M. and by 6 P.M. everything had to be done. It was the beginning of the Passover festival. During those three hours, permission in writing had to be granted by Pilate for the body of Jesus to be removed from the cross, the body had to be taken down from the cross, and the body had to be transported from Golgotha to Joseph of Arimathea's tomb. Likewise, the argument against the anointing is that it would have been incongruous to anoint the body without first washing it. Then what about the spices which John's Gospel (19:39f) says were brought to anoint Jesus' body? It has been suggested that the spices were dry blocks of aromatics and were packed around the body as antiputrefacients. If this were the case, then the body would have remained firm and straight. This point supports the clear image on the Shroud. Nevertheless, the Scripture arguments are filled with some controversies.

The Official Church Position

While the Church recognizes the findings of scientists, physicians, historians, photographers and others to be very interesting, the Church has not defined it as a matter of faith (dogma). Will it ever do so? Probably not because there will always be unanswered questions about its authenticity. Can one privately believe that the Shroud is the burial cloth of Jesus? Yes. Is it essential to the Roman Catholic faith? No.

Comment

Although the authenticity of the Shroud is not universally accepted by scholars, its acceptance today is more common than it was in the past. The progress of science and scholarship has added a new interest in the Shroud. Perhaps the one test that can determine once and for all the authenticity of the Shroud is the Carbon 14 test which measures the remaining amount of the radioactive isotope in organic matter. Permission for this test was denied by the Vatican in 1978 to the scientists of the American scientific commission. What would be required for the test is a very small piece of cloth from the Shroud. While this test is not absolutely conclusive for an exact date, it would be able to determine whether the Shroud is a first century cloth or not. Certainly this fact would strengthen the authenticity of the Shroud's case. Is the Shroud a six hundred year fake or a nineteen hundred year old authenticity? In the Roman Catholic Church there is a new wave of openness. The ultimate decision rests with the present Holy Father, John Paul II. Will he grant permission for a piece of the Shroud to be subjected to the Carbon 14 test? The future knows the answer.

Summary

1. The Shroud of Turin is 14½ feet long and 3½ feet wide and is reported to be the burial cloth of Jesus.

2. The Shroud is presently located in the Royal Chapel of St. John the Baptist at Turin, Italy.

3. An Italian photographer, Secondo Pia, photographed the Shroud for the first time in 1898.

4. Professors Vignon and Delage presented to the French Academy of Science on April 21, 1902, a report saying that the man of the Shroud was Jesus Christ.

5. The historical documentation of the Shroud can be verified for the last six hundred years. Prior to the fourteenth century, it can only be loosely reconstructed.

6. Prior to the fourteenth century, the Shroud seems to have been in Edessa (now Urfa, Turkey), and Constantinople, Turkey and France.

7. From the fourteenth century, the Shroud can be traced to Lirey and Chamery, France. Eventually, it came to Turin in the sixteenth century where it is today.

8. Crucifixion was a severe and harsh method of punishment by the Romans for all non-Romans. They adopted this practice from the Persians.

9. Occasionally the Romans inflicted crucifixion on "new citizens," namely people who were either emancipated slaves or provincials.

10. Three types of crosses were used by the Romans, namely the X form, the T form and the form on which Jesus was crucified.

11. The length of time for death on the cross depended on the amount of blood lost by scourging. It could be a few hours or days.

12. The man of the Shroud of Turin shows that the nailing was done through the wrist which would have supported the body.

13. The crowning of thorns was done to Jesus because he was accused of being a king. Normally this feature was not part of the crucifixion scene. The man of the Shroud shows bruises around the head.

14. Jewish burial customs included washing and anointing the corpse. This custom was prevalent in the New Testament times.

15. According to the Synoptic Gospels (Mt 27:59; Mk 15:46; Lk 23:53) the body of Jesus was wrapped in a Shroud. John's Gospel states that Jesus was wrapped in a linen cloth and a small piece of cloth was placed on the face.

16. Greek philologists say that the Greek words of John do not mean two separate pieces of cloth but one piece of cloth.

17. Only two evangelists (Jn 12:7; Lk 23:53) mention that spices were brought to the tomb for anointing.

18. Myrrh and aloes were the traditional spices for anointing the body of a deceased person.

19. The image of the man of the Shroud shows severe bruises around the head, shoulders and the entire body. Also it shows that he was crucified.

20. Jesus was scourged outside the Roman praetorium, then crowned with thorns.

21. All four evangelists state that Jesus was crucified. However, they do not indicate whether it was done by nails or ropes.

22. The man of the Shroud indicates that he suffered a wound around the rib cage on the right side. Jesus' side was pierced by a lance.

23. Many experts believe that the bloodstains on the Shroud came from real blood, not paint. Men like Drs.

Willis, Bucklin, and Barbet support this idea. Dr. Walter McCrone says that these "bloodstains" are merely iron oxide residue from paint.

24. The scorching theory is basically rejected because it is very difficult for modern technology, let alone medieval technology.

25. Dr. Max Frei, a Swiss criminologist, supports the authenticity of the Shroud because of the identification of dust particles belonging to halophyte plants common to the desert regions of the Jordan Valley of the first century.

26. The Shroud's negativity was perhaps created accidentally or deliberately by some early artist.

27. The bloodstains on the Shroud have not been demonstrated to belong to the first century.

28. Dr. McCrone's position cannot be confirmed by experimentation.

29. Dr. Frei's position supports the authenticity of the Shroud.

30. Professor Haralick's photographs cannot conclusively prove that coins were placed on the eyes of the man in the Shroud.

31. The scientist Joseph Nickell's technique of "scorching" with myrrh and aloes would not have been known in the medieval times.

32. Tradition says that Jesus' body was washed. However, the Gospels do not support this theory.

33. The official position of the Roman Catholic Church is that the Shroud is not a matter of faith (dogma). Catholics may accept it or reject it. They may hold it privately if they wish.

34. The Carbon 14 test could greatly support the authenticity of the Shroud.

35. Pope John Paul II alone can give permission for a piece of the Shroud to be subjected to the Carbon 14 test.

Discussion Questions

1. Describe the Shroud of Turin. Where is it located today?

2. What did Secondo Pia discover?

3. Explain the report of Drs. Vignon and Delage.

4. Briefly summarize the historical aspect of the Shroud prior to the seventeenth century.

5. What happened to the Shroud during the Second World War?

6. Who owned the Shroud? Who owns it today?

7. Who practiced crucifixion in ancient days?

8. Who were subjected to the crucifixion penalty?

9. Discuss the nails or ropes procedure for crucifixion.

10. What concession was granted to the Jews who were crucified?

11. What importance did the Jews place on burials?

12. Discuss the differences between the Synoptic Gospels (Matthew, Mark and Luke) and John's Gospel concerning the Shroud of Jesus.

13. Which Gospels mention the spices for the burial of Jesus?

14. What is myrrh? Name the spices used for Jesus' burial.

15. Discuss the many bruise similarities between the man of the Shroud and Jesus.

16. Discuss the position of Drs. Willis, Bucklin and Barbet.

17. Why do some experts believe that the bloodstains on the Shroud are real bloodstains?

18. Why has Dr. McCrone's position been questioned?

19. What is the scorching theory?

20. What did Dr. Max Frei discover?

21. Discuss the weak points of photographs, bloodstains, coins and tradition concerning the authenticity of the Shroud.

22. What is the official position of the Roman Catholic Church regarding the Shroud?

23. Why would the Carbon 14 test help to authenticate the Shroud?

24. Why is Pope John Paul II important for the authenticity of the Shroud?

Suggested Readings

Pierre Barbet, *A Doctor at Calvary*. New York: P.J. Kennedy & Sons, 1953.

Robert Bucklin, "The Shroud of Turin: A Pathologist's Viewpoint," *Legal Medicine Annual*, 1981.

Werner Bulst, *The Shroud of Turin*, Milwaukee: Bruce Publishing Co., 1957.

James Freeman, *Manners and Customs of the Bible*. Plainview: Logos International, 1972.

Robert Haralick, *Analysis of Digital Images of the Shroud of Turin*. Blacksburg: Virginia Polytechnic Institute, 1983.

John Heller, *Report on the Shroud of Turin*. Boston: Houghton Mifflin Co., 1983.

Berna Kurt, *Criminal Report about the Shroud of Jesus Christ*. Stuttgart: Real Buchverlag Co., 1965.

Willard Libby, *Where Was the Shroud Before the Fourteenth Century?* Chicago: University of Chicago Press, 1955.

John McKenzie, *Dictionary of the Bible*. Milwaukee: The Bruce Publishing Co., 1965.

Joe Nickell, "The Turin Shroud: Fake? Fact? Photography?" *Popular Photography* 85, November 1979 pp. 97–99, 146–147.

Samuel Pellicori and Mark Evans, "The Shroud of Turin Through the Microscope," *Archaeology*, Jan.–Feb. 1981, pp. 32–43.

K. Stevenson, *Verdict on the Shroud*. Ann Arbor: Servant Books, 1981.

Paul Vignon, *The Shroud of Christ*. New Hyde Park: University Books, 1970.

John Walsh, *The Shroud*. New York: Random House, 1983.

Robert Wilcox, *The Shroud*. New York: Macmillan Co., 1977.

Ian Wilson, *The Shroud of Turin*. Garden City: Doubleday, 1978.

7

The Dead Sea Scrolls

Since the discovery of the Dead Sea Scrolls in 1947, there has been speculation that Jesus may have been a member of the Dead Sea Community (Qumran) or that his Last Supper resembles the Dead Sea community's sacred meal. These scrolls indicate that John the Baptist, a cousin of Jesus, was probably a member of the community. Naturally, these two ideas are of great interest to the Christian community. In light of the importance of this issue, we will examine the Dead Sea discovery and its implications for Christians today. This discovery created a revolutionary impact on the world, especially the Christian and Jewish communities. For Jews, it makes audible the voices of their long dead comrades. For Christians, it has revealed the spiritual home of Jesus.

The Discovery

In the spring of 1947, two shepherds of the Bedouin Taamireh tribe discovered several stone jars in the caves of the Judean wilderness, near the northwestern shores of the Dead Sea, about sixteen miles east of Jerusalem.

This discovery was soon acclaimed as the greatest archaeological discovery of the twentieth century. It shed light on the writings of a Jewish group of people, the Essenes, who lived at a place called Qumran and who probably came into contact with Jesus. It opened a new era in Jewish-Christian dialogue.

From the spring of 1947 to the present time, scholars have examined and translated the material found: scrolls and fragments of several hundred manuscripts, including biblical and non-biblical literature. The job has been difficult because of the fragile condition of the scrolls and the scarcity of competent biblical scholars. Nevertheless, the work continues and presently this much can be said about the discovery.

The Dead Sea Scrolls

There are two complete scrolls of the Book of Isaiah; a commentary on the prophet Habakkuk; a manual of discipline with regulations governing the community, admission of candidates, conduct, punishment of infractions and ritual prescriptions; a collection of Thanksgiving hymns; a scroll on the War of the Children of Light against the Children of Darkness; a scroll on the Book of Genesis, and thousands of fragments from all the books of the Old Testament except the Book of Esther.

These scrolls reveal the devotion to the study of the law of Moses. For them, the law meant a way of life including positive and negative prohibitions. Their literature contains many legalistic rules, especially concerning the observance of the sabbath and Jewish feasts. They observed the calendar of the Book of Jubilees which Jesus may have followed. There are prescriptions for ritual

washings and observance of sacred meals on special occasions. Finally, annual examinations, punishments and
expulsions from the community underscore the serious
application of their discipline to their life in the community.

The Community

The scrolls were written between 150 B.C. and A.D.
150 by Jews, generally believed to be Essenes. The Essenes lived at the Qumran site, approximately ten miles
south of Jericho and sixteen miles east of Jerusalem. Its
second occupation lasted from 4 B.C. to A.D. 68.

The Essene community, a Jewish sect, consisted of
priests and lay people (men, women, children) who were
pursuing a well-organized communal existence in strict
dedication to the will of God. Because of their dedication
to the laws of God, they were earnestly repentant for
their sins. Since they believed they were the last generation in the "last days" of the earth, they were conscious
of the need of a moral washing and purification. The
sanctification of their meals also was significant to the Essene community. Both of these practices are mentioned
in their Manual of Discipline and Messianic Rule scroll—
two pieces of the Dead Sea literature.

The Synoptic Gospels contain much about the Pharisees and the Sadducees who lived in the time of John the
Baptist and Jesus. However, there is no mention of the Essenes who were contemporaries of both John and Jesus.
Some biblical scholars say that Jesus was probably an Essene. The discovery of the Dead Sea Scrolls now gives us
some information about a group of Jews who lived in the

time of Jesus. Since John worked in the Jordan area where these people lived, he no doubt came into contact with them. Consequently, Jesus most likely knew of them and mingled with them. The Dead Sea literature makes one aware that there was a Jewish sect whose members were striving for perfection by studying the Scriptures in order to find and do the will of God. The New Testament writings have a similar message. Like the Christians, this Essene sect taught and recorded their teachings. However, unlike the early Christians, they were exclusive, secretive, esoteric and priest-led.

Jesus' Message and the Essene Message

There are differences between the messages of Jesus and the Dead Sea Scrolls messages. This Essene sect was led by a priest who played a very large role in the life of people. Apparently, nothing could take place without the mediation of the priest. There is no such clericalism in the New Testament writings. The Essenes were meticulously concerned about ceremonies and rituals. Jesus was not. At his Last Supper he did not adhere to all Passover requirements. The Essene messages were basically consistent with the Old Testament. The human being's salvation is centered in the covenant grace of God. The Essenes emphasized the need for forgiveness and purification to keep or to restore the relationship between God and his creature. Their emphasis was primarily on ritual purification. Jesus' emphasis was basically an interior conversion. They disassociated themselves from sinners. Jesus mingled with all types of people, the sinner as well as the unclean. They abandoned the temple worship in Jerusalem. Jesus worshiped regularly at the Temple. They preached only to Jews. Jesus' message was for Jew and non-Jew. Their leader, the Teacher of Righteousness, claimed to be the last prophet. Jesus claimed to be the Son of God.

Jesus' Last Supper

Christians heard, perhaps for the first time, of a communal meal at Qumran that was messianic in character. According to the Dead Sea literature, members were required to observe their rules until the Messiah appeared. This fact has led many to the premature inference of seeing the Dead Sea sacred meal as a prototype of Jesus' Last Supper. According to the Gospels, Jesus used the elements of bread and wine as symbols of his body and blood. It is this fact that gives special meaning to his use of the bread and wine. Even as everyone present at the meal ate the bread and drank the wine, so would all share in the atonement of his death, of his body and his blood to be shed.

This understanding of the bread and wine at the Last Supper pointing to the death of Jesus is not paralleled in the Dead Sea literature. It is impossible to avoid this interpretative significance which can be traced back to Jesus himself. There is no such theological significance given to the Essene sacred meal. In the final analysis, it is the person of Jesus that makes his meal significantly different from the Essene sacred meal. It might be added that any coincident resemblance between the Essene sacred meal and Jesus' Last Supper might be the common descent of both from the rite of Passover.

Jesus at Qumran

Since the Synoptic Gospels speak of Jesus being in contact with John the Baptist who came into contact with the Essenes at Qumran, Jesus probably met the Qumran Essene community. Second, Jesus himself went into the desert area. The Gospels say that he fasted for forty days in the desert. Some biblical scholars speculate that he stayed at this community to rest and pray. Since they were very good living people, he would have been attracted to them. Third, the Gospels are silent about Jesus' "hidden years" (between the ages of twelve and thirty). Could he and Mary have spent those years at Qumran? The Qumran community welcomed widows and orphans who were religious Jews. Jesus and Mary would have been ideal candidates. Christian tradition assumes that Jesus worked as a carpenter in Nazareth during those years. While the Qumran theory may be improbable, it is not impossible. Certainly we can say that Jesus preached in the area of Qumran. He probably met some Qumran Essenes through John the Baptist or others. The Qumran area might be called part of the spiritual lore of Jesus. Finally, the Dead Sea literature is silent on the matter.

Insights from the Dead Sea Scrolls

These scrolls have given new insights into three areas, namely, messianism, the Jewish calendar, and John the Baptist. All three areas are directly related to Jesus. Therefore, they are important in the study of Jesus.

First, messianism is faith in the power and will of God to save his people consistently developed in Judaism.

Throughout Jewish history, Israel learned that salvation could not be achieved through cultural and political institutions, but only through the intervention of God. The obstacle to salvation was humanity's refusal to accept it and so God had to intervene. Thus is seen the reference to a personal human agent of deliverance to be sent by God. It is interesting that this element is also present in the Dead Sea literature, apart from normative Jewish literature. However, the Dead Sea Scrolls give evidence that some Jews of Jesus' time expected two Messiahs. Both would be human persons, a military messiah and a priestly messiah. The idea of the divinity of a Messiah is absent from the literature. The Dead Sea Scrolls give meaning to Jesus' controversy with the Pharisee who resented his teaching that he is the Son of God and is the Messiah the Jews have been expecting for such a long time.

Second, the Qumran Essenes followed a calendar different from that of official Judaism during the time of Jesus. They used a solar calendar. As a result, the Qumran Essenes celebrated feasts and fasts on different days from the rest of the Jewish community. This information has led to a possible solution of an ancient problem—disagreement between the Synoptic writings and John's Gospel as to when Jesus celebrated his Last Supper. In the Synoptic accounts, the Last Supper is called a Passover. In John's Gospel, the Last Supper is celebrated before the Passover. This might mean that Jesus and his disciples followed the Qumran Essene calendar calculation of the time of the Passover rather than the official calendar at Jerusalem. It is a possible solution to harmonize the Synoptic accounts with the Gospel of John. What seems important is that another calendar besides the official Jewish calendar was used during the time of Jesus.

Third, John the Baptist, a cousin to Jesus, was born in a small village approximately twenty miles west of Qumran. More significant, however, is the fact that John's ministry was conducted in the general vicinity of Qumran. He preached and taught fewer than ten miles from Qumran. It is impossible to believe that he was ignorant of the Qumran Essene community within the very area in which he lived and worked.

John's message centers on his proclamation of the imminence of the judgment of God and the appearance of the Messiah. The Qumran Essene sect also expected this judgment and that the evil one would be destroyed by fire. The good would be saved because they had a washing purification accompanied by a moral purification. Both Qumran and John the Baptist were adamant about the necessity for repentance. Although there are differences, there are striking similarities. The Christian is faced with the real possibility that John was either a member of this community or at least aware of it. Therefore, he was probably influenced in some way in his preaching and teaching. The Qumran Essene community forms the background of John's ministry. It is from this group or movement that John emerges as an independent and individual figure. John's connection with the community makes Jesus' association with them stronger.

Similarities and Dissimilarities

There are parallels in content and expression in the Dead Sea Scrolls and the New Testament writings. Since the Scrolls pre-date the New Testament writings, there is no evidence that the New Testament writings quote directly from the Dead Sea Scrolls. There are some parallel expressions, thoughts and practices. This factor does not indicate that the New Testament writings are dependent on the Scrolls. Since the Qumran Essene community was essentially secretive, no one would have accessibility to them except their own members. It is also highly improbable that some Qumran Essenes left the sect and became Christians and thus divulged these beliefs and practices to the Christian writers.

In both, God is an active God, the Creator and Judge of all peoples.

In both, God demands the obedience of humans, and the future rests in God's hands.

Both writings indicate that they are living in the last days of the world.

Both writings believe that the imminence of God demands immediate repentance.

The difference between the two groups is primarily in the two founders: the Teacher of Righteousness and Jesus of Nazareth.

The Teacher of Righteousness who considered himself the last prophet claimed that God had entrusted him with some final messages. On the other hand, Jesus taught that he was the Messiah, the Son of God, and that through him all would be saved.

Also, there are differences between the message of Jesus and the Qumranian teachings.

According to the Qumran literature, the sect was led by a priest who played a very large role in the life of the Qumranians. Apparently nothing could take place without the mediation of the priest.

There is no such clericalism in the Synoptic Gospels. In fact, Jesus was not a priest.

The Qumran community was especially concerned

with ceremonies and rituals. These were important to them.

From the account of the Last Supper, it is apparent that Jesus was not a ritualist, for he did not adhere to the Passover requirements at this meal.

The Qumranians disassociated themselves from sinners; Jesus associated with all men, including sinners, while after the Qumranians abandoned the Temple worship, they withdrew to the wilderness of Judea. They had sacred meals which it is believed may have substituted for the temple sacrifices.

From the Synoptic accounts, it seems that Jesus differed with the priests of the temple, but he continued to worship there.

Finally, Jesus, who celebrated his Last Supper on this earth with his closest friends, designated the bread and wine as symbols of his body and blood. He told his apostles to repeat this action after he had left them.

The Qumran Essenes were commanded to hate their enemies and shun all sinners. Jesus' command was to love all, rich and poor, sinner and saint, Jew and non-Jew.

The Dead Sea Scrolls believed in militarism. In their documents, there are prayers for wars. One is commanded to destroy all one's enemies. Jesus' message was one of peace. One must love one's enemies.

The Qumran Essenes were selective and secretive. Their teachings were reserved for themselves. If one wanted to join their group, there were strict rules of probation and acceptance. In many cases, two years was the normal probation period. Jesus' teachings were not secret. He preached openly. He invited everyone to follow him.

The Qumran Essenes expected two messiahs, a military leader and a religious leader. They would usher in the final days of the world. Jesus speaks of himself as the new Messiah. He claims to be the Son of God.

In conclusion, the Dead Sea Scrolls have given Christians another source of information about the vocabulary, beliefs, and customs of a Jewish sect that lived in the time of Jesus.

Comment

The discovery of the Dead Sea Scrolls has afforded Jews and Christians fresh stimulus for the study of Jesus and normative Judaism. The Qumran Essenes and Jesus were contemporaries. For the Jews, the Qumran Essene practices of baptism and the sacred meal are a source of new material against the normative Judaism of that era. For the Christians, the Qumran Essene practices provide new background material in the study of John the Baptist's baptism and Jesus' Last Supper. Therefore, a tolerance toward one another's religious practices should lead to a fruitful dialogue. The objective of dialogue is not superficial consensus or the finding of the most acceptable common fact. It does not lead to the dilution of all convictions for the sake of false harmony but to the enrichment of all in the discovery of new dimensions of truth.

In conclusion, three points can be made: (1) The two bodies of literature (the Dead Sea Scrolls and the New Testament writings) have a different historical perspective. They seem to be in different circles since not a single person, date, or event is mentioned in common. (2) The two bodies of literature are similar in religious perspective. Both have common sectarian movements in Judaism that share eschatological expectations. (3) The Dead Sea

Scrolls provide valuable material for the study of the times of Jesus.

Finally, the Qumran Essenes were deeply religious Jews who were searching to find the will of God. Their literature is enlightenment for anyone in search of God. A famous biblical scholar, Millar Burrows, said: "It is as though Jesus and the Qumranians drew water from the same spring but carried it in different vessels."

Summary

1. The Dead Sea Scrolls were discovered by Bedouin Arabs at Qumran in 1947.

2. Qumran is located sixteen miles east of Jerusalem on the northwestern shores of the Dead Sea.

3. The Dead Sea Scrolls are ten scrolls, manuscripts and tens of thousands of fragments of scrolls. They are biblical and non-biblical literature.

4. The Dead Sea literature reveals many legalistic rules and regulations for observance of the sabbath, Jewish feasts, moral washings and sacred meals and all books of the Old Testament except Esther.

5. The Dead Sea Scrolls were written between 150 B.C. and A.D. 150.

6. The people who produced the Dead Sea Scrolls are called Essenes, who were a Jewish sect of priests and lay persons (men, women, children).

7. Two special practices (sacred meals and moral washings) are contained in the Manual of Discipline and Messianic Rule scrolls.

8. The Dead Sea literature reveals a Jewish sect that was living in the time of Jesus and believed they were living in the final days of the world.

9. The Dead Sea literature adds to the Christian knowledge of Jesus' times.

10. The primary difference between Jesus' and the Essene messages was the emphasis on interior-exterior condition of the person and the type of people. Jesus emphasized the interior conversion while the Essenes emphasized the exterior ritualistic attention. Jesus appealed to all types of people (Jews, non-Jews), unclean, rich, poor. The Essenes appealed to Jews who were not sinners.

11. The Essene sacred meal had a messianic element, but did not have the same meaning of Jesus' Last Supper.

12. Jesus' Last Supper gives special meaning to the bread and wine, namely, that it is his body and blood.

13. It is possible that Jesus spent some time at Qumran during his early teenage and adult years.

14. Qumran is part of the spiritual home of Jesus.

15. Three insights (messianism, calendar, John the Baptist) come from the Dead Sea Scrolls for Christianity.

16. Messianism in the Dead Sea Scrolls reveals that the Essenes were expecting a military Messiah and a priestly Messiah.

17. The Essenes used the solar calendar which was not used by the ordinary Jew of Jesus' time.

18. The solar calendar has given a possible biblical solution to the contrasts of the Synoptic and John's Gospel accounts of Jesus' Passover Meal.

19. John the Baptist, a cousin of Jesus, preached in the area of Qumran.

20. John the Baptist may have been a member of the Qumran Essene community or at least been aware of it.

21. There are similarities and dissimilarities of content and expressions in the Dead Sea Scrolls and the New Testament writings.

22. The similarities are an active God, living in the final days of the world and repentance.

23. The primary difference is the founders of the communities (Jesus and the Teacher of Righteousness).

24. Other differences are clericalism, ritualism, sinners, temple worship, and sacred meals.

25. The Dead Sea Scrolls' discovery affords new dialogue between Christians and Jews.

26. The Dead Sea Scrolls and the New Testament literature have a different historical perspective but a similar religious perspective.

Discussion Questions

1. Briefly explain the discovery of the Dead Sea Scrolls.

2. Name the Dead Sea Scrolls.

3. Name some of the Essene community's rules.

4. When were the scrolls written?

5. Where is Qumran?

6. What relationship exists among the Essenes, John the Baptist and Jesus?

7. Who are the Qumran Essenes?

8. State two differences between Jesus' and the Essene messages.

9. What main common idea do the sacred meals and the Last Supper have?

10. What makes Jesus' Last Supper unique?

11. Could Jesus have been at Qumran?

12. Explain briefly three main insights from the Dead Sea Scrolls.

13. State three similarities and ten dissimilarities between the Dead Sea Scrolls and the New Testament writings.

14. Is there a value for Jews and Christians in studying the Dead Sea Scrolls?

15. What about the historical and religious perspective of the Dead Sea Scrolls and the New Testament literature?

Suggested Readings

Matthew Black, ed. *The Scrolls and Christianity.* London: The Talbot Press, 1969.

Matthew Black, *The Scrolls and Christian Origins.* California: Scholars Press, 1983.

Raymond E. Brown, "The Dead Sea Scrolls and the New Testament," in James H. Charlesworth, ed. *John and Qumran.* London: Geoffrey Chapman, 1972, 1-8.

Millar Burrows, *More Light on the Dead Sea Scrolls.* New York: The Viking Press, 1958.

James H. Charlesworth, ed., *John and Qumran.* London: Geoffrey Chapman, 1972.

Roland De Vaux, *Archaeology and the Dead Sea Scrolls.* London: Oxford University Press, 1973.

A. Dupont-Sommer, *The Jewish Sect of Qumran and the Essenes.* New York: The Macmillan Company, 1956.

Charles T. Fritsch, *The Qumran Community.* New York: The Macmillan Company, 1956.

Josef T. Milik, *Ten Years of Discovery in the Wilderness of Judaea.* Naperville: Alec R. Allenson Inc., 1959.

William LaSor, *The Dead Sea Scrolls and the New Testament*. Grand Rapids: William B. Eerdmans, 1972.

Cecil Roth, *The Dead Sea Scrolls: A New Historical Approach*. New York: W.W. Norton and Company, Inc., 1965.

Cecil Roth, *The Historical Background of the Dead Sea Scrolls*. New York: Philosophical Library Inc., 1959.

Ethelbert Stauffer, *Jesus and the Wilderness Community at Qumran*. Philadelphia: Fortress Press, 1964.

Edmund Wilson, *The Dead Sea Scrolls 1947–1969*. New York: Oxford University Press, 1969.

Walter Wink, *John the Baptist in the Gospel Tradition*. Cambridge: University Press, 1968.

8

Jesus' Human Knowledge

The question of Jesus' human knowledge is important for all Christians. Each age has investigated the problem. We are no less curious than our predecessors. The Christian faith states that Jesus Christ was truly God and truly man. It says further that Jesus had two natures, two wills, two intellects (human and divine) which were integral and perfect within one person. Therefore, he had to possess divine and human knowledge together at all times.

The problem is the human knowledge of Jesus. Since Jesus possessed divine knowledge at every moment of his human existence, was his human knowledge unlimited or limited? If the former is true, then he was not completely human. If the latter is true, then he was not fully divine. This dilemma is examined under four areas: (1) the New Testament writings; (2) three major general councils and the twentieth century papal statements; (3) theological insights; (4) comment.

The New Testament

Jesus being God and man had a divine and a human knowledge. Both types are a dogma of the Catholic faith. That means if one knowingly and deliberately denies a dogma of the Church, one is excluded from the official membership of the Catholic Church. What is not defined explicitly is how Jesus' human knowledge operated. Was it an acquired, infused or beatific knowledge? Was it limited or unlimited? Jesus' words and actions are recorded in the New Testament writings. A look at these accounts will give an insight into the problem.

The Gospels mention the events of Jesus' life which reveals his human knowledge. When he is twelve years old, he astonishes people by his knowledge (Lk 2:40–47). During his ministry, all are wondering at his teachings (Mt 7:28–29). He knows distant things (Mk 13:32). He reads the hearts of people (Lk 6:8; Mk 2:6–8). He predicts the future (his passion, the fall of Jerusalem) (Jn 1:14). He asks questions and wonders at the answers he is given (Mk 5:31; Jn 11:34; Mt 8:10).

There are indications that Jesus' human knowledge was unlimited. Several examples emphasize this point. First, Matthew's account (9:22) of the woman afflicted with a hemorrhage for twelve years who touches Jesus' garment and his healing power went out from him says that Jesus immediately identifies the woman. Second, John's account (6:5) says that while Jesus asked Philip where they could find enough bread to feed a large crowd, Jesus knew all the time what he was going to do. He merely tested Philip. Third, John's account (6:71) mentions that Jesus knew that some of his disciples would be unfaithful. Fourth, several Gospel accounts (Mk

2:6–8; Lk 9:46–47; Jn 2:24–25) attribute to Jesus the ability to know what others are thinking. Fifth, Mark (14:13–14) and Luke (22:10) mention that Jesus knew of events taking place somewhere else.

There are indications that Jesus' human knowledge was limited. These examples demonstrate this point. First, Luke's passage (2:52) says that Jesus "progressed steadily in wisdom." Second, Mark (2:26) says that Jesus identified the high priest, Abiathar, at the time of David who entered the house of God and ate the holy bread. Historically speaking, Ahimelech, not Abiathar, was the high priest. Third, Mark (5:4) and Matthew (12:43–45) show that Jesus confused demon possession with epilepsy and insanity. Fourth, Mark (13:32) records Jesus as saying, "as to the exact day or hour, no one knows it, neither the angels in heaven nor even the Son, but only the Father."

Of special interest is whether or not Jesus' human knowledge (limited or unlimited) showed conscious awareness of his messiahship. This idea can be understood when the messianic titles are examined. Did Jesus accept these titles? Did he ever identify himself with any title?

For six hundred years before Jesus, the Jews expected the Messiah (the anointed one of God). He would be the successor of King David who would restore freedom once again to the Jewish nation. In Jesus' time, people had different ideas of what the Messiah would be. The Essenes expected two messiahs, one religious, one military. The Pharisees looked for a religious leader. The Zealots awaited a military man. In any case, this Messiah would be an earthly person, not a divine being. Certainly Jesus was aware of these ideas during his time. The messiahship was expressed in several ways or titles such as the Messiah, the Son of God, the Son of Man, and the Prophet. The Messiah title is mentioned in two Gospel passages. Mark's account (8:27–33) speaks of Peter's assertion that Jesus is the Messiah and relates Jesus' rebuke of Peter. Obviously Jesus understood Peter's statement. He rejected it because of the prevalent Jewish concept of the Messiah. Basically, it was a political-military concept of restoring the freedom of the Jews. Matthew's account (26:62–68) mentions the preliminary investigation of Jesus before the Sanhedrin (Jewish senate). Jesus' reply to the high priest's question "Are you the Messiah?" was "You have said so." This statement would be understood either as a noncommital answer or as an outright denial. One must conclude that Jesus never directly used the term Messiah of himself. Had he done so, he would have supported the current popular notion of the Messiah among his listeners.

The Son of God title is never used by Jesus in speaking of himself. In Judaism, the Son of God title was applied to angels. Sometimes it was used for the Jewish people as a whole. Other times it signified a devout Jew. It was never used for a human being meaning he was divine. However, John's Gospel used it six times for Jesus. The Synoptic Gospels (eleven times in Matthew, seven times in Mark, nine times in Luke), the Acts of the Apostles (two times), John's letters (seventeen times), and the Pauline letters (eighteen times) used the term for Jesus. Biblical scholars point out that this term expresses rather the faith of the early Christians than the personal self-consciousness of Jesus as the Son of God. Although the Synoptic Gospels never present Jesus as explicitly calling himself the Son of God, he is clearly portrayed as being conscious of being sent by God as a divine agent. The evangelists recognize all this after Jesus' resurrection when he appeared to them as the Son of God.

While it must be admitted that Jesus never used this title for himself, he was conscious of a unique Sonship with God. His words and deeds show a Father-Son relationship.

The Son of Man title normally meant "man" collectively, that is mankind. During Jesus' time it took a special meaning, "the man" or "a man." In the New Testament writings the term is used eighty-two times for Jesus. Jesus accepts the term for himself. It is the only title he used in speaking of himself. All the Synoptic writers use the term with Jesus' power to forgive sin in the story of the paralytic of Capernaum (Mk 2:10f), with Jesus' authority over the Sabbath (Mk 2:28f), with his sitting at the right hand of God in Jesus' testimony before the Sanhedrin (Mk 14:62f), with Jesus saying that the Son of Man has no place to lay his head (Mt 11:19), and with Jesus saying that the Son of Man came to seek and to save the lost (Lk 19:10). The Synoptic accounts use the term to stress Jesus' divinity. On the other hand, John's Gospel uses the term to stress Jesus' humanity. For example, Jesus will be given power to judge mankind because he is "a Son of Man." In John (6:62) the Son of Man (Jesus) is clearly pre-existent insofar as he came down from heaven, so he ascends to the place from which he came.

The Prophet title is never used by Jesus of himself. In the Hebrew language, the word means "one who speaks for God." The title was given to some persons in early Jewish history. Men like Samuel, Nathan, Elijah, Isaiah, Jeremiah and Ezekiel prophesied. Were there prophetic figures in the time of Jesus? Yes. John the Baptist was the most outstanding. Was Jesus himself a prophet? The title is applied to him by others (Mt 16:24; Mk 6:15; 8:28; Lk 7:16; Jn 4:19; 6:14; 7:40). But it is never applied by Jesus to himself or by the evangelists which suggests that Jesus did not claim the title although he did not reject it. The unusual personage of Jesus makes it difficult to fit him into any of the charismatic prophets and religious leaders of Jewish history. He was not a scribe but yet he is often addressed as rabbi. He was not a priest. He speaks for God yet he never uses the prophetic formulas. He speaks on his own authority. There was a Jewish belief that a final prophet would appear before the coming of the Messiah. Jesus implicitly rejected this identification by hinting strongly that John the Baptist was the final prophet.

But did Jesus understand himself as the prophet? There are two passages in which he compares his fate with that of a prophet. Mark (6:4) says, "And Jesus said to them: 'A prophet is not without honor, except in his own country and among his own kin, and in his own house.'" In Luke (13:33) Jesus says, "Nevertheless, I must go on my way today and tomorrow and the day following; for it cannot be that a prophet should perish away from Jerusalem." In neither passage does Jesus use the title for himself. He is quoting a proverb or popular notion. In other words, without using "prophet" as a self-designation. Jesus indicates that he understood his role in prophetic terms. Yet he did not use the title for himself.

From the New Testament writings, we can conclude that Jesus' human knowledge was limited and unlimited at times. Some New Testament passages indicate that Jesus had moments of ignorance and error. Yet an examination of Jesus' words about the presence of the Kingdom of God, his moral teachings, the call to follow him, his healings, his miracles and his forgiveness of sins demonstrate his God-Man awareness. Also his sayings about his death show his understanding of his mission. There is a unique human consciousness about himself.

The General Councils and Papal Statements

Having explored the New Testament writings about Jesus' human knowledge, the evidence of the three major general councils of the Church will be examined.

In order to understand the force of a general council, a brief historical background is necessary. A general council is a gathering of the bishops of the Church called together by the Pope (in the ancient Church and in the Eastern part of the Empire, the emperor summoned a council) in order to discuss questions of faith or morals or Church discipline or guidance.

The Roman Catholic Church has been in existence almost two thousand years. It was founded by Jesus Christ and it was Jesus who appointed Peter as its first leader (Pope). As the Church grew in the world, it encountered problems and it had to face them. From Peter to the present Pope John Paul II, each Pope has had the responsibility of Jesus' command, "All power is given to me in heaven and on earth. Go, therefore, teach all nations, baptizing them in the name of the Father, and the Son, and the Holy Ghost, teaching them to observe all things whatsoever I have commanded you; and behold I am with you all days even to the consummation of the world" (Mt 28:18–20).

Because of human problems and doctrinal controversies, the authorities of the Church have had to settle these matters. In its long history, the Church has had twenty-one general or ecumenical councils. However, it was not until the fourth century (325) that the Church had its first general council.

Until the fourth century, "councils" were really groups of bishops of small areas who met to discuss pastoral practice, or to decide on the authenticity of the books of the Bible. A "general" or "ecumenical" council is supposed to have representatives from all Christian communities. This has always been an ideal not actually accomplished because doctrinal or political disputes often prevented some groups from being represented at the councils. There are twenty-one councils recognized by the Roman Catholic Church. This means that the teachings of these councils are binding on Catholics dogmatically. If a Catholic knowingly and deliberately denies a dogma, he or she is excluded from the official membership of the Church.

The Council of Nicea (325) condemned the denial of the divinity of Jesus made by Arius, an Alexandrian priest. This heresy began in Africa and Egypt. Arius held that Jesus was merely a human being. Athanasius, a bishop of Alexandria, led the battle against this idea. After much discussion, the Council adopted the following Creed: "We believe in one God, the Father, the Almighty, maker of heaven and earth, of all that is, seen and unseen. We believe in one Lord, Jesus Christ, the only Son of God, eternally begotten of the Father, God from God, Light from Light, *true God from true God,* begotten, not made, one in Being with the Father. Through him all things were made. For us men and for our salvation he came down from heaven: by the power of the Holy Spirit he was born of the Virgin Mary, and *became man.* For our sake he was crucified under Pontius Pilate; he suffered, died, and was buried. On the third day he rose again in fulfillment of the Scriptures; he ascended into heaven and is seated at the right hand of the Father. He will come again in glory to judge the living and the dead, and his kingdom will have no end. We believe in the Holy Spirit, the Lord, the giver of life, who proceeds from the Father and the Son; with the Father and the Son he is worshiped and glorified. He has spoken through the prophets. We believe in one holy catholic and apostolic Church. We acknowledge one baptism for the forgiveness of sins. We look for the resurrection of the dead and the life of the world to come."

In essence, the Council decree formally stated that Jesus is truly the Son of God and that he became man.

Although the Nicean Creed affirmed the divinity of the Son, it remained silent about the distinction between the Father, the Son, and the Holy Spirit. This problem was discussed and settled by the Council of Chalcedon (451). However, in between the Council of Nicea and the Council of Chalcedon, another problem had to be settled. It was the Nestorian heresy. Nestorius, the bishop of Constantinople, stated that Mary was the Mother of Jesus' human nature, but was not the Mother of his divine nature.

The Council of Ephesus (431) was called and condemned Nestorius. The fathers of this Council actually made no new formula of belief. Rather, they settled a belief that was already contained in the Nicean Creed. Approximately two hundred fathers issued the following statement: "One and the same is the eternal Son of the Father and the Son of the Virgin Mary, born in time after the flesh; therefore, she may rightly be called Mother of God." Ephesus' importance was to stress the fullness of Jesus' humanity.

The Council of Chalcedon condemned the monophysitism which taught that Jesus had one nature (not two, human and divine as the Church had taught). The final formula or Creed was expressed in this way: "Therefore, following the holy Fathers, we all with one voice teach that it should be confessed that our Lord Jesus Christ is . . . truly God and truly man . . . of one substance with the Father as to his Godhead, and at the same time of one substance with us as regards his manhood . . . recognized in two natures, without confusion, without separation, not as parted into two persons, but one and the same Son." Jesus has a human nature and a divine nature. The Chalcedon decree made clear that Jesus was truly a man in all things except sin. While the Creed of Chalcedon reflects the teachings of Scripture and the early tradition of the Church, it helped to spur on future theological reflection.

Have these three major general councils given any real insight into the operation of Jesus' human knowledge? No. Their main considerations were basic. They were concerned with these main points: (1) there is one person in Jesus; (2) Jesus had two natures (divine and human); (3) there is a complete union of Jesus' divine and human natures; (4) Jesus was truly the God-man who suffered, died and rose from the dead for humanity's sins and salvation. They did not discuss the finer points of Jesus' humanity such as interaction of his divine and human knowledge.

What about the papal statements on this problem? There are three important pronouncements by the Popes of the twentieth century. First Pope Pius X in 1907 in his document, *Lamentabili*, rejected the idea that Jesus' human knowledge was limited. Second, Pope Benedict XV in 1918 issued a Holy Office decree saying it was unsafe to say that Jesus may not have had the beatific vision at all times. Third, Pope Pius XII in 1943 in his document, *Mys-*

tical Body of Christ, declared that Jesus had the beatific vision at all times.

What type of authority do the general councils and papal statements possess? Briefly, the general council decrees are dogmas (infallible statements) and must be accepted by all Catholics. Papal statements are fallible statements and can be rejected but with great danger to one's faith. The Church is a society composed of the Pope, bishops, clergy and laity. All are obliged to help one another to fulfill their temporal and spiritual destiny. All share in the teaching authority of the Church but in different ways. Parents are the primary teachers of their children. The Pope possesses the highest teaching authority in the Church. Bishops and priests have the authority to teach and preach the messages of the Gospels. The theologians have the authority to teach and speak responsibly. The laity have the authority to share their knowledge and ability with the entire Christian community. All Church members must exercise their authority mutually and respectfully.

How does the Church exercise this authority? There are three ways: (1) infallible teachings; (2) non-infallible teachings; (3) private opinions.

First, the infallible teachings (dogmas) are stated in the Apostles' Creed. The General Councils of Nicea, Ephesus and Chalcedon must be accepted under penalty of expulsion from the membership of the Church. For our purpose, we have seen that their statements were basic points about the divinity and humanity of Jesus. These statements are infallible and must be accepted. Since they did not make specific remarks about the interaction of Jesus' human and divine knowledge, we are free to discuss and probe this problem.

Second, there are certain Church teachings which

are classified as non-infallible teachings. Yet these are authoritative teachings of the Church. An example of this type of teaching are the papal statements. Because of the Church's vast wisdom and knowledge, Catholics would be unwise to disregard these teachings. We have discussed the papal statements on Jesus' human knowledge. Keeping in mind what has been said about these teachings, one can explore, discuss and debate the problem of Jesus' human knowledge—whether it is infused, acquired or beatific—and also if Jesus' human knowledge exhibited ignorance and error at times.

Third, there are private teachings such as opinions of theologians. How are these teachings to be accepted? Catholics must weigh the importance of these opinions in light of the person's reputation. These teachings are not binding on the Catholic community. Yet, a person should be open to listening to new ideas.

Theological Insights

Until now, we have considered the problem of Jesus' human knowledge from the viewpoint of the New Testament writings, the general Church councils and papal statements. We will consider the insights of the greatest medieval theologian, Thomas Aquinas and several contemporary Roman Catholic theologians on this question. The primary function of theologians is to give insights from their research.

A few ancient theologians struggled with this problem of Jesus' human knowledge. However, it was not until the Middle Ages that a breakthrough on this issue came. Thomas Aquinas proposed two ideas, namely, an acquired knowledge and an infused knowledge. By acquired knowledged he meant that Jesus learned through daily experiences as all human beings do. Jesus gained his knowledge of talking, reading, carpentry and so forth in a normal human manner. Aquinas based this theory on the New Testament writings. For example, Luke's account (2:52) says that Jesus "advanced in wisdom." The Pauline Hebrew letter (5:8) says that Jesus "learned obedience from the things that he suffered." This idea was not shared by other medieval theologians like Scotus and Bonaventure. However, Aquinas' theory finds supporters among contemporary Catholic and non-Catholic theologians. By infused knowledge Aquinas meant that certain aspects of Jesus' human knowledge would not be acquired through ordinary sense experience, but would be directly implanted by God.

A third type of knowledge, the beatific vision in Jesus, has been proposed by other theologians. The beatific vision means that there is a face to face vision of God. That Jesus had such knowledge is perhaps implied in the New Testament writings as: "Not that anyone has seen the Father except him who is from God; he has seen the Father" (Jn 6:46); "I speak what I have seen with my Father" (Jn 8:35). At the Last Supper, Jesus said, "Just Father, the world has not known you but I have known you" (Jn 17:25). This theory is logical since Jesus is both divine and human. His human knowledge had to receive its source from the original source (his divinity). Though this beatific vision is fitting, it offers a number of problems. If Jesus had the beatific vision, how could he have truly suffered his passion? Furthermore, how could he have been ignorant of anything? Yet Jesus did suffer and did learn from experience.

In summary, the traditional view of Jesus' human knowledge has been that Jesus had the beatific vision of

God from the first moment of his human existence. In addition to his acquired knowledge through human experience, he received infused knowledge from God.

Several contemporary theologians have offered new insights into this traditional theory. H. Riedlinger says that the human Jesus had an historical vision of God while the divine Jesus had the beatific vision. Both are joined in the person of Jesus. It means that Jesus as a man lived fully in history, subject to the course of everyday events. He experienced novelty in human encounters, was moved and led by unexpected events. Thus it was only in the unveiling of historical events that Jesus saw clearly that path he would have to take. In other words, Jesus' human knowledge was subject to ignorance and error. Bernard Lonergan explores the consciousness idea— what it means to be conscious of something. For him, the human Jesus was conscious, at least in a non-reflective way of his divine personality. Karl Rahner suggests that the beatific vision does not mean that the human Jesus continually saw the essence of God. He says that Jesus' human knowledge developed gradually. Therefore, Jesus' self-consciousness grew gradually. Well, what is the answer? Perhaps two points must be kept in mind: (1) consciousness is not the same as express knowledge; (2) at times it seems that Jesus is ignorant about certain points, but the Gospels portray him as a man who acts and speaks for God. In conclusion, some theologians are convinced that because of the hypostatic union with God the Father, Jesus could not have been limited in what he knew. Other theologians will argue that because Jesus was truly human except in sin, his knowledge would be gradual. Therefore, it remains an open question. Whatever possible solutions are offered, they are theories, not

facts. Perhaps as our knowledge of the human being de-
velops, there will be new insights into how human knowledge operates. That in turn will give new insights into
Jesus' human knowledge.

We must remember that Jesus was the most unique
person, both God and man. Therefore, this problem
about Jesus' knowledge will still remain a great mystery.

Comment

We have explored one of the most fascinating aspects of Jesus, his human knowledge. Because Jesus
Christ is truly man, his humanity is a fact of human obser-
vation. We believe that Jesus was truly a perfect man. He
had a complete human nature including a human body.
His human nature was complete with all the human
senses. He was hungry. He was tired. He wept. He slept.
He talked. He thought. Yet, being God, he possessed a
unique knowledge, a divine and human knowledge. His
divine knowledge was infinite. Was his human knowledge infinite? Several New Testament passages indicate
ignorance and error in Jesus. Also there are passages
which indicate that he was not consciously aware of his
divinity. What are the explanations? Can we say that the
Gospel writers did not clearly express themselves? Perhaps Jesus conformed to the confusing religious views of
his time. Perhaps Jesus deliberately suppressed his divine
knowledge at times. Biblical and dogmatic theologians
are divided on whether Jesus' human knowledge was limited or unlimited. The medieval theologians and the
twentieth century papal statements favor the unlimited
theory. Some modern theologians have embarked on the

limited knowledge theory. They use terms such as historical vision, non-reflective consciousness and gradual self-consciousness.

Two final notes should be made. First, the official Church has not made an infallible statement on this issue. Second, the brilliant and respected Catholic biblical scholar, Father Raymond Brown, made a very significant statement about this problem of Jesus' human knowledge.

Raymond Brown says that Jesus speaks of himself in a special relationship to God and claims to be God's unique Son. While some Gospel passages do not necessarily show that Jesus was consciously aware of his messiahship, it may be due to a lag between consciousness and express knowledge. One may be vividly conscious of something long before one finds a reasonably adequate way to express that consciousness. Furthermore, Brown asserts that neither the hypostatic union nor other privileges extended to Jesus necessarily endowed him with extraordinary knowledge. Rather, some sort of intuition or immediate awareness of what he was happened, and a communicable way had to be acquired gradually. Therefore, Brown distinguishes between self-consciousness and expressed knowledge. Consequently, this idea would explain the apparent ignorance and error on the part of Jesus. And it does not make him any less the God-Man.

Summary

1. Jesus possessed two natures, two wills, two intellects in one person.

2. Jesus' divine and human knowledge is a dogma of the Catholic Church.

3. The operational aspect of Jesus' human knowledge was unlimited.

4. Certain Gospel accounts indicate that Jesus' human knowledge was unlimited.

5. Luke (2:52), Mark (2:26; 5:4; 13:52) and Matthew (12:43–45) indicate that Jesus' human knowledge was limited.

6. A special aspect of Jesus' human knowledge (limited or unlimited) was his conscious awareness of his messiahship.

7. The Messiah means the anointed one of God.

8. The messiahship is expressed in several titles such as Messiah, the Son of God, the Son of Man, and the Prophet.

9. The Messiah title in Jesus' time basically meant a political-military term. Jesus rejected the title for himself.

10. The Son of God title was never used by Jesus for himself but was used by the early Christians.

11. Jesus' words and deeds show his unique relationship with his heavenly Father.

12. The title Prophet was never used by Jesus of himself, but was applied to him by the Gospel writers.

13. The term Prophet meant the one who speaks for God.

14. Jesus indicates that John the Baptist was the last Prophet.

15. Mark (6:4) and Luke (13:33) indicate that Jesus compared his fate with that of a prophet.

16. Some New Testament passages indicate that Jesus' human knowledge was limited and unlimited.

17. A general council basically has the Church representatives from all parts of the world.

18. The teachings of the general councils are dogmatically binding on all Catholics.

19. The Council of Nicea (325) condemned the denial of Jesus' divinity made by the Alexandrian priest Arius.

20. The Council of Nicea specifically states that Jesus became man.

21. The Council of Ephesus (431) condemned Nestorius, the bishop of Constantinople who denied that Mary was the Mother of the divine Jesus.

22. The Council of Ephesus stressed the full humanity of Jesus.

23. The Council of Chalcedon (451) stated that Jesus was truly God and truly man.

24. The three major general councils did not give information on how Jesus' human knowledge operated.

25. Pope Pius X, Pope Benedict XV and Pope Pius XII issued papal statements supporting the unlimited theory of Jesus' human knowledge.

26. The general council statements are infallible teachings of the Catholic Church.

27. Papal pronouncements are fallible teachings of the Catholic Church which must be taken seriously.

28. The Catholic Church exercises its authority in three ways: (1) infallible teachings (dogmas); (2) fallible teachings; (3) private teachings.

29. The medieval theologian, Thomas Aquinas, suggested that Jesus' human knowledge was acquired and infused.

30. Acquired knowledge means that Jesus learned through daily experiences.

31. Infused knowledge means that it was implanted by God.

32. Beatific vision knowledge means that one has a continuous vision of God.

33. If the human Jesus had the beatific vision, then he could not have suffered the way a human being normally does.

34. The traditional view on Jesus' human knowledge is that Jesus possessed the beatific vision, acquired and infused knowledge.

35. H. Riedlinger suggests that Jesus had historical vision.

36. B. Lonergan suggests Jesus was conscious in a non-reflective manner.

37. K. Rahner suggests that Jesus' human self-consciousness grew gradually.

38. Jesus' human knowledge issue remains an open question today.

39. The biblical theologian, Raymond Brown, proposes a distinction between self-consciousness and expressed knowledge.

Discussion Questions

1. Give examples of Jesus' human knowledge.

2. Give four examples from the Gospels supporting the unlimited and limited theory about Jesus' human knowledge.

3. What did the Messiah term mean in the time of Jesus?

4. What could Jesus have meant by his reply to the high priest's question about his messiahship?

5. Briefly indicate the number of times in the New Testament writings that the Son of God term is used for Jesus.

6. Define the terms Son of Man, Son of God and Messiah.

7. Who was the most outstanding prophet?

8. Which title did Jesus not claim but not reject either?

9. Did Jesus ever compare himself to a prophet?

10. What can we conclude from the New Testament evidence about Jesus' knowledge being limited and unlimited?

11. What is a general council of the Catholic Church?

12. How binding are the general councils on Catholics?

13. Give three main ideas from the Council of Nicea statement.

14. Who was condemned by the Council of Ephesus?

15. Which Council stressed the fullness of Jesus' humanity?

16. What did the Council of Chalcedon condemn? What did it firmly support?

17. When did the Councils of Nicea, Ephesus and Chalcedon meet?

18. Did the three major councils add any information on the operation of Jesus' human knowledge?

19. Briefly discuss the three ways the Church exercises its authority. Which type is binding under penalty of being excluded from the Catholic Church?

20. Who was Thomas Aquinas? What was his contribution to Jesus' human knowledge problem?

21. What does acquired, infused and beatific vision knowledge mean?

22. Discuss briefly the theories of the theologians Riedlinger, Lonergan and Rahner.

23. What has Raymond Brown contributed to solve this issue?

Suggested Readings

Raymond Brown, *Jesus God and Man*. New York: Macmillan Publishing Co., 1973.

Rudolf Bultmann, *Theology of the New Testament*. New York: Charles Scribner's Sons, 1955.

John and Denise Carmody, *Contemporary Catholic Theology*. San Francisco: Harper & Row Publishers, 1980.

Joseph Fitzmyer, *A Christological Catechism—New Testament Answers*. New York: Paulist Press, 1982.

Reginald Fuller, *The Foundations of New Testament Christology*. New York: Charles Scribner's Sons, 1965.

Joseph Grispino, *The Bible Today*. Notre Dame: Fides Publishers , Co., 1971.

Ernest Kasemann, *New Testament Questions of Today*. Philadelphia: Fortress Press, 1979.

Dermot Lane, *The Reality of Jesus*. New York: Paulist Press, 1975.

Richard McBrien, *Catholicism*. Minneapolis: Winston Press, 1981.

Stephen Neill, *What We Know About Jesus*. Grand Rapids: William B. Eerdman's Publishing Co., 1973.

Gerald O'Collins, *In Search of Human Jesus*. New York: Corpus Books, 1969.

Michael Schmaus, *Dogma 3: God and His Christ*. New York: Sheed and Ward, 1971.

9

Special Biblical Questions about Jesus

The collection of writings which is known as the Bible (Old and New Testaments) was written within a thousand year period (900 B.C.–A.D. 100). Having been completed by the end of the first century, they are almost two thousand years old. Written originally in the Hebrew and Greek languages, they have been translated into various languages. To understand them properly, they must be studied in their original languages and cultural settings.

For well over a hundred years biblical scholarship has engaged itself in the pursuit of special questions about Jesus. Because of new scientific knowledge of biblical times, Catholic and Protestant biblical scholars cite new insights. New information about ancient biblical customs, languages, archaeology, and literature is now available for further biblical studies.

Our attention is drawn to six questions which are asked frequently by many people. Did Jesus have brothers and sisters? Do the Gospels record the exact words of Jesus? Did Jesus believe in the devil as a person? What about the virginal birth of Jesus? Can non-Christians be saved without Jesus? Finally, did Jesus predict the time of the end of the world?

Did Jesus Have Brothers and Sisters?

Various passages of the New Testament refer to the brothers and sisters of Jesus. "Is not this the carpenter, the son of Mary, the brother of James, Joseph, Jude and Simon? And are not also his sisters here with us?" (Mk 6:3; Mt 13:55–56). John's Gospel (2:12; 7:3–5) and the Acts of the Apostles (1:14) say "his brothers." Paul calls James "the brother of the Lord" (Gal 1:19). The Synoptic Gospels (Mt 12:46–50; Mk 3:21–25; Lk 8:19–21) speak of "his mother and his brothers" who came to see Jesus as he was preaching. The Gospels (Mt 1:20 and Lk 1:34) state that Mary was a virgin and that Jesus was conceived through the power of the Holy Spirit. Finally, Luke (2:7) says that Mary gave birth to her "firstborn son."

Since the New Testament writings were written in Greek, it is important to examine the Greek words *adelphos*, which is used primarily for a physical brother, and *adelphe*, for a physical sister. Yet these words have been used to denote a close relation, a companion, a friend and even a fellow-official in Greek literature. Therefore, which meaning did the New Testament writers intend? The argument has to be settled in favor of Jesus not having any physical brother or sister. Why? Because of the early tradition of the Christian Church. The early Christian writers speak of the perpetual virginity of Mary. In other words, Mary was a virgin and remained a virgin after the birth of Jesus. Jesus was conceived by the special power of the Holy Spirit and was the only child of Mary. Secondly, the New Testament writings themselves do not offer any substantial evidence that Mary had other children besides Jesus.

In conclusion, Roman Catholics and many Protestant Christians hold the belief that Jesus was the only child of Mary. A minority of Protestant Christians accept the idea that Mary may have had other children after the birth of Jesus. Orthodox Christians understand the brothers and sisters of Jesus as children of Joseph by an earlier marriage. The evidence for these last two statements is rather shallow. The majority of Christians accept the traditional belief of their early Christian predecessors that Mary was a virgin before and after the birth of Jesus and that Jesus did not have any physical brothers or sisters.

Do the Gospels Record the Exact Words of Jesus?

What are the very words of Jesus in the Gospel accounts? Which of the sayings attributed to Jesus in the Gospels were actually spoken by him? This biblical problem has been the subject of recent investigation. Because of biblical studies of literary forms (metaphors, allegories, hyperboles, fables, parables), heuristics (the search for meaning), languages, customs and archaeology, biblical scholars are examining this problem about the exact words of Jesus. Before answering this question as to whether or not the Gospels record the exact words of Jesus, it would be helpful to understand the background to the formation of the Gospels.

Generally, Catholic and Protestant biblical scholars recognize a threefold level behind the written accounts of the Gospels. The *first level* is the words and deeds of Jesus. Jesus walked and preached in various areas of Palestine. He visited and preached his message in many Palestinian towns and cities. He spoke and healed people. Rich and poor, religious and non-religious, young and old people heard him. He picked twelve men, took them about with him, and trained them so that they could carry on his work. The *second level* is the preaching and teaching of the apostles. These twelve men preached the message of Jesus which has come to be known as the "good news" (Gospel). Their prime aim was to proclaim Jesus Christ the Son of God who brought salvation to all peoples. The *third level* is the actual written stage. The Gospels were written roughly between A.D. 60 and 100. The Gospel writers (evangelists) recorded the material which the followers of Jesus had reflected on and recorded orally. The evangelists (Matthew, Mark, Luke, John) were Christians writing for Christians, composing a record which reflected the sayings and actions of Jesus. The evangelists were not eyewitnesses in our modern sense of the word. Mark was not one of the apostles. He was a disciple of Peter from whom he obtained much of his knowledge about Jesus. Luke was a Greek convert of Paul and had never seen Jesus. The Greek Gospel of Matthew, as we have it, is based on a previous Aramaic copy. Matthew was an apostle of Jesus and had seen and heard Jesus. John's Gospel was written either by the apostle John or his disciple. In any case, the evangelists did not write a biography of Jesus, though they wrote some biographical material. Their prime aim was the proclamation of Jesus' good news.

In handling their material, they adapted it to the situation of their listeners. Within each Gospel we will sometimes have the very words of Jesus, sometimes a paraphrase of his sayings and sometimes a dramatization of Jesus' statements. Yet, while the Gospel writers did not give an exact transcript of the words Jesus used, they recorded a substantially accurate version of what Jesus said.

Those who are still preoccupied with knowing "the exact words of Jesus" may use one fairly definite method. That is, since Jesus spoke Aramaic his exact words would have to have Aramaic words. When the Greek translation of certain words or expressions can be retranslated back into Aramaic, we can generally presume that they are "the exact words of Jesus."

In conclusion, this problem is best summarized in the statement of the noted Jesuit biblical scholar, John McKenzie: "The question of the very words of Jesus remains, consequently, alive in modern interpretation. The primitive Church apparently saw nothing in this question. They preserved the memory of the words of Jesus and they applied these words to their own situation in life. They felt that this was what should be done with the words of Jesus, and they were incapable of sharing our nearly pathological concern about the exact words of Jesus. They felt that the words of Jesus should live in the life of the Church and not be embalmed in the mausoleum of literary remains."

Did Jesus Believe in the Devil as a Person?

In the world of Jesus, the devil was believed to be the cause of sickness as well as sin. The idea that demons were responsible for all moral and physical evil had penetrated deeply into Jewish religious thought after the Babylonian exile. In Babylonia, the Jews were subjected to Persian notions of demons and devils. When the Jews returned to their homeland, these Persian ideas influenced Jewish thought. The ancient Persian religion believed that there were two supernatural beings of almost equal power, one good and the other evil. In Jesus' time, the devil (Satan) was regarded by the Jews as head of a kingdom of evil. Jesus was accused by the Jewish scribes of using the power of Satan or Beelzebub in driving out demons from people.

The Synoptic writers (Matthew, Mark, Luke) say that Jesus was tempted by Satan before he began his public ministry. Jesus replies to the suggestions by quoting Old Testament texts. Jesus expels devils by a simple command (Mt 12:28). In the Gospels the work of Jesus is presented as overcoming evil. His exorcisms over evil spirits show his divine power. Luke's and John's accounts of Judas' betrayal of Jesus is considered the work of the devil. Jesus' entire ministry is a constant battle with the forces of evil.

What can we conclude from these readings about Jesus' expressions of the devil's existence? We are not sure that Jesus' statements can be used to establish the physical existence of the devil as a person. Many biblical scholars state that Jesus did not believe in the devil as a person. Rather he used the popular language of his time to talk about the real existence of evil. While several papal statements have said that the devil exists, the official Church has never declared it as a dogma of the faith. What the Church has dogmatically taught is that there is evil in the world. It really exists.

Father Grispino, a biblical scholar who holds a licentiate in Sacred Scripture from the Pontifical Institute in Rome, has asserted: "We may state that the evidence of Scripture merely shows that the Israelites (Jews) of the Old Testament popularly held to a belief in evil spirits, but this belief was never part of their official body of revealed truths. Jesus and the writers of the New Testament assumed these popular notions into their teachings about evil and God's power to conquer it without ever explicitly teaching the existence of the devil. The early and medieval Church took these presuppositions about the existence of the devil uncritically and added to the scanty scriptural notions a rather involved body of speculation which later generations of Christians assumed to be truth revealed in Scripture. Therefore, it seems unnecessary for committed Christians to hold to the belief in devils as an object of faith (personal existence). It must be made clear that a denial of the devils as personal spiritual beings is not thereby a denial of real evil in the world that affects us personally, both individually and collectively."

What About the Virginal Birth of Jesus?

The perpetual virginity of Mary is a dogma of the Catholic faith and was explicitly stated in the fifth century by the General Council of Ephesus (431). Not until the fifth century did the Church have any real problem with its traditional belief in the virginal birth of Jesus. Nestorius, a priest who became the patriarch of Constantinople in 428 taught that Mary was the Mother of the human person Jesus, but not of the divine Jesus. He was condemned by the General Council of Ephesus. The Council said, ". . . for in the first place no common man was born of the holy Virgin: then the word thus descended upon him; but being united from the womb itself he is said to have endured a generation in the flesh in order to appropriate the producing of his own body."

Succeeding councils have emphasized the virgin birth of Jesus. For example, the First Lateran Council

(649), the Council of Trent (1545–1563), and the Second Vatican Council (1962–1965) specifically mentioned this idea. These general council statements are articles of faith for all Catholic Christians. They have preserved the main thinking of the early Christians. To deny any one of them would be a serious problem. That is, one becomes a heretic.

There are also numerous papal statements on this issue. Although these statements are not all of equal importance, they must be taken seriously. They do reflect the Church's thinking on this matter.

All of the general council and papal statements are based on the New Testament writings which clearly say that Jesus was conceived in the womb of the virgin Mary by the power of God, without the intervention of a human father. The Gospels of Matthew and Luke are primarily interested in Mary's conception of Jesus. Matthew's Gospel (approx. 70–75) makes several references to Mary. They are: (1) the account of the virginal birth of Jesus (1:18–25); clearly, Jesus has no human father in his conception; it speaks of Mary as being a virgin before the conception of Jesus and the power of the Holy Spirit as responsible for the conception of Jesus in her womb; (2) the account of the magi and the flight into Egypt (2:7–23); (3) the account of Mary and the apostles listening to a speech of Jesus in Nazareth (12:46–50); (4) the account of people who say, "Is not his mother called Mary?" (13:55). Luke's Gospel (approx. 70–75) basically reiterates Matthew's references to Mary's conception of Jesus. He speaks of the annunciation by the angel Gabriel to Mary of her conception of Jesus (1:26–38), the experience of Mary and her cousin Elizabeth (1:39–52), and the birth of Jesus (2:1–20). Basically, then the New Testament writings of Matthew and Luke establish that Mary is the mother of the human and divine Jesus, and was divinely favored in the redemptive work of God by bringing Jesus into the world.

In conclusion, Father McBrien, the former president of the Catholic Theological Society of America, stated: "The virginal conception has been understood from the very beginning as a statement about Jesus first, and about Mary only secondarily. Through this belief, the Church clearly taught that Jesus is from God, that he is unique, that in Christ the human race truly has a new beginning, that the salvation he brings transcends this world, and that God works through human instruments, often weak and humble instruments at that, to advance the course of saving history. If, in denying the historicity of the virginal conception, one is also denying such principles as these, then one has indeed moved outside the boundaries of the Christian, and certainly the Catholic, tradition. However, a more traditional understanding of the doctrine remains an integral part of belief and devotion for a great many Catholics."

Can Non-Christians Be Saved Without Jesus?

The New Testament writings (Lk 8:17; Acts 16:30f; Rom 10:9; 1 Cor 1:21) say that belief in Jesus is necessary for salvation. Luke says: "The ones along the path are those who have heard; then the devil comes and takes away the word from their hearts so that they will not believe and be saved" (8:10). To believe is to accept a promise with confidence. In a word, one can say that belief is a commitment. Throughout the New Testament, Jesus calls his followers to a commitment to his ideas. Salvation is Jesus' key idea.

The official teaching of the Church on the question of non-Christian salvation has been clearly stated by the Second Vatican Council (1962–1965) in several of its documents:

1. The Constitution of the Church (#16) says, "Those also can attain everlasting salvation who, through no fault of their own, do not know the Gospel of Christ or his Church, yet sincerely seek God and are moved by grace to strive by their deeds to do his will as it is known to them through the dictates of conscience. Nor does Divine Providence deny the help necessary for salvation to those who, without blame on their part, have not yet arrived at an explicit knowledge of God, but who strive to live a good life, thanks to his grace."

2. The Decree on Ecumenism (#3) says, "Moreover, some, even very many of the most significant elements or endowments which together build up and give life to the Church itself can exist outside the visible boundaries of the Catholic Church"; also (#4): "Today in many parts of the world, under the inspiring grace of the Holy Spirit, multiple efforts are being expended through prayer, word and action, to attain that fullness of unity which Jesus Christ desires."

3. The Declaration on the Relationship of the Church to Non-Christian Religions (#35) says, "But the plan of salvation also includes those who acknowledge the Creator. . . ."

And so, the non-Christian can be saved. This positive answer rests on the notion of grace. Grace is God's presence, which is total and complete, even though it may reveal itself in many different ways at different times. It has always existed; therefore, the primitive and ancient peoples, who knew nothing of Jesus and the one God, certainly experienced God's grace. Like anyone, their salvation depended on how they cooperated with it. Obviously, they had to deal with it in light of their knowledge and experience of God. Likewise, the same statement holds for the non-Christian religions of today, like Zoroastrianism, Hinduism, Buddhism, Islam and Judaism.

In conclusion, Father Richard McBrien, the noted theologian, said "God is available to all peoples widely differentiated as they are by time, by geography, by culture, by language, by temperament, by social and economic conditions, etc. Revelation is received according to the mode of the receiver, and the response to revelation (religion) is necessarily shaped by that mode of reception."

Did Jesus Predict the Time of the End of the World?

Essentially, this question is rooted and intermingled in three ideas: first, the nuclear age today; second, the justice of God; third, biblical prophecies. First, we are well aware that the total and complete destruction of the world is now possible. Practically every nation in the world possesses hydrogen bombs, atomic war missiles, etc. The world stands on the brink of a world inferno. Will it happen? When will it happen? How will it happen? All three questions plague humanity. The horrible reality of nuclear war has prompted peace marches in cities all over the world. Young and old alike demonstrate and pray for peace as though the final hour of civilization is now at hand. And so, people ask: "When?" More and more people are convinced that time runs out in a nuclear arms race.

Second, the justice of God links the second idea to the first. Although the word "justice" takes complex meanings in the Old and New Testaments, one clear sense emerges: that justice is determined through the righteousness of God. Through the judgment of God, this justice of God is bound to the covenant. In the Old Testament, the Jews hold the covenant of God. In the Old Testament, the judgment of God at times takes forms both vindictive (Jgs 1:27) and punitive (Ez 5:7–15; Gn 18:25; Dn 7:9–11). In the New Testament, the expansion of the covenant by Jesus is with all peoples. In the New Testament, the judgment of God at times is associated with condemnation (Mt 5:22; Lk 12:58; Rom 5:16; Jn 3:18). Since the covenant demanded a bilateral agreement, the violation of it meant a punishment by one of its partners. And so, many incidents in the Scriptures state that God "punishes" those who violate the covenant. Therefore, there is the thinking that the justice of God will demand that he should end the world because of the many violations of his laws.

Third, and perhaps more predominant in the minds of people, are the biblical prophecies about the end of the world.

In the Old Testament, the exile period (740–540 B.C.) speaks of the most traumatic time for the Jews. They lost their independence. The occupation forces of the Babylonians and Assyrians subjected the Jews. Even after this exile period, they were subjected to other foreign rulers, to heavy taxation, and to limited religious freedom.

For the Jews, fire was the element by which Yahweh would destroy the wicked: the cities of Sodom and Gomorrah (Gn 19:24), the enemies of Israel (Am 1:4f), the wicked in general (Is 1:22; Ez 22:17–22). Eventually, we see that the Jews slipped into the question we ask today: "How long, O Lord?" as voiced by the psalmist. The Book of Daniel, in particular, is filled with symbols of Yahweh destroying the world soon.

In the New Testament, the notion of fire as God's weapon to destroy the world continues. John the Baptist speaks of it (Mt 3:10; Lk 3:9). Jesus also speaks of destruction by fire, "but on the day when Lot went out from Sodom fire and brimstone rained from heaven and destroyed them all. . . . So will it be on the day when the Son of Man is revealed. . . . Will he delay long over them (the righteous)? I tell you, he will vindicate them speedily" (Lk 17:29–18:7).

Again, the most vivid illustration of God's judgment is in the Book of Revelation, or, as it is also called, the Apocalypse. It speaks of the end of the present age and the coming of the new age (4:1; 22:5), the judgment of God against his enemies (14:6; 20:15), the final battle (20:1–10), and so on.

All these illustrations from the Bible have caused people to believe that the end of the world is going to take place by fire, and soon. What can we say in light of these writings? They were written in their time zone, speaking with the symbols and terms of the people of that time. They were speaking about things that were going on then, not future events. What we are saying, then, is that we do not know when the world is going to end. While there are evidences that God will end it with fire, and soon, there are other examples to prove that we are not sure when it will end. We can reassure ourselves that we do not know when or how the end of the world will take place by reading Jesus' words, "No one knows the day or the hour, not the angels, not even the Son, only the Father" (Mk 13:32–37).

Comment

These six biblical questions are being asked by many Catholics today. The answers to these questions are proposed by Catholic biblical theologians in full communion with Rome. The answers reflect solid investigation in light of current biblical information. The role of biblical theologians is to research, reflect and present insights into problems about Jesus. At the same time, their primary responsibility is to serve the community of believers by proclaiming clearly the faith of the Church today. In the years ahead, this faith may be refined, qualified and reformulated in light of new knowledge. But the members of the Catholic community have a right to be told by Catholic theologians what the official Church proclaims as Catholic teaching at the moment.

Summary

1. The Synoptic Gospels (Mt 12:46–50; Mk 3:31–25; Lk 8:19–21) speak of Jesus' "mother and brothers."

2. The Greek word *adelphos* means primarily a physical brother, while *adelphe* means a physical sister.

3. The words *adelphos* and *adelphe* can also mean a close relative, companion, friend, or fellow-official.

4. A majority of Catholics and Protestants believe that Jesus was the only Son of Mary.

5. Orthodox Christians believe that Joseph may have had children from a former marriage.

6. Within every Gospel we have sometimes the very exact words of Jesus, sometimes a paraphrase of his sayings, and sometimes a dramatization of Jesus' statements.

7. Aramaic words may indicate the exact words of Jesus.

8. The primitive Church was more interested in the memory of the words of Jesus rather than his exact words.

9. There are three levels behind the written Gospels: the words and deeds of Jesus, the apostles' teaching and preaching, and the written accounts.

10. The evangelists were not eyewitnesses in the modern sense of the word.

11. The ancient Persian religion believed in two supernatural powers: one good and the other evil.

12. Jesus' entire ministry was a constant battle with the forces of evil.

13. The official teaching of the Church does not state that the devil exists as a person. Papal statements do.

14. Some biblical scholars believe that Jesus used the popular notion of the devil in his speech.

15. The virginal birth of Jesus means that Jesus was born of the body of the Virgin Mary.

16. The virginal birth of Jesus has always been held by the Church. It was officially stated by the General Council of Ephesus in the fifth century.

17. Several general councils teach the virginal birth of Jesus as a matter of faith.

18. Matthew's and Luke's accounts specifically mention the virginal birth of Jesus.

19. A denial of the virginal birth of Jesus excludes one from membership in the Catholic faith.

20. The official teaching of the Church on the question of non-Christian salvation is contained in the Constitution on the Church, the Decree on Ecumenism, and the Declaration on the Relationship of the Church to Non-Christian Religions.

21. Non-Christians can be saved without Jesus.

22. Non-Christian religions experience the saving grace of God.

23. The answer to the question about the end of the world is contained in the nuclear age today, the justice of God and biblical prophecies.

24. Many Scripture passages state that God will punish those who violate his laws.

25. The Book of Daniel of the Old Testament in particular is filled with symbols of God destroying the world soon.

26. The Book of Revelation of the New Testament in particular speaks of the end of the present age, the coming of the new age, and the final battle.

27. Jesus did not predict the time of the end of the world.

Discussion Questions

1. Explain the Greek words *adelphos* and *adelphe*.

2. What is the position of Catholics, Protestants and Orthodox Christians on the question of Jesus' "brothers and sisters"?

3. Give three Scripture references to support the idea that Jesus did not have any physical brothers and sisters.

4. What is the general conclusion about the "exact words of Jesus"?

5. What is Father McKenzie's position about the "exact words of Jesus"?

6. What are the three levels behind the written Gospel accounts?

7. Name the evangelists. When did they write the Gospels?

8. Did the Jews believe in the existence of the devil? Explain.

9. What is the official Church position on Jesus' belief in the existence of the devil as a person?

10. Briefly state Father Grispino's position on the devil.

11. What does the virginal birth of Jesus mean?

12. Explain Matthew's and Luke's position on the virginal birth of Jesus.

13. What is the key idea of Father McBrien's position on the virginal birth of Jesus?

14. What do the New Testament passages (Lk 8:17; Acts 16:30f; Rom 10:9; 1 Cor 1:21) say about salvation?

15. Give one reference from Church pronouncements about salvation.

16. Briefly state why non-Christians can be saved without Jesus.

17. What does the Old Testament say about the end of the world?

18. Give examples from the New Testament which give an indication of the end of the world.

19. Which statement of Jesus gives a clue to the end of the world idea?

Suggested Readings

R. Brown, J. Fitzmyer, and R. Murphy, eds., *The Jerome Biblical Commentary*. New Jersey: Prentice-Hall, Inc., 1968.

Raymond Brown, *The Virginal Conception and Bodily Resurrection of Jesus*. New York: Paulist Press, 1973.

Joseph Fitzmyer, *A Christological Catechism—New Testament Answers*. New York: Paulist Press, 1982.

Joseph Grispino, *The Bible Now*. Notre Dame: Fides Publishers, Inc., 1971.

Richard McBrien, *Catholicism*. Minneapolis: Winston Press, 1981.